DYKE DRAMA

by LESLIE LANGE

DYKE DRAMA

YOUR GUIDE TO GETTING OUT ALIVE

alyson books
los angeles

MANUFACTURED IN THE UNITED STATES OF AMERICA.

THIS TRADE PAPERBACK ORIGINAL IS PUBLISHED BY ALYSON PUBLICATIONS,
P.O. BOX 4371, LOS ANGELES, CALIFORNIA 90078-4371.
DISTRIBUTION IN THE UNITED KINGDOM BY TURNAROUND PUBLISHER SERVICES LTD.,
UNIT 3, OLYMPIA TRADING ESTATE, COBURG ROAD, WOOD GREEN,
LONDON N22 6TZ ENGLAND.

FIRST EDITION: FEBRUARY 2005

05 06 07 08 09 a 10 9 8 7 6 5 4 3 2 1

ISBN 1-55583-893-6

CREDITS
- COVER PHOTOGRAPHY BY FRANK HERHOLDT/STONE/GETTY IMAGES AND BERT HARDY/HULTON ARCHIVE/GETTY IMAGES.
- COVER DESIGN BY MATT SAMS.
- INTERIOR ILLUSTRATIONS ON PAGES 5, 19, 24, 28, 40, 52, 63, 73, 89, 154, 160, 185, 204, 209, AND 222 BY ELLEN FORNEY.

To those who suffer...

And to Foofoo Garblepie Nightlight,
the cat I would have...
if I weren't allergic.

.

Contents

Introduction

This book's publication was delayed for a season, a miscalculation that occurred when I first started talking to people about the subject of dyke drama and was met with all kinds of enthusiasm: "Oh, God, honey, I could sit down with you, tell you my life story, and you'd have the whole thing done and wouldn't even need to talk to anybody else!" And it wasn't just my mother who had this opinion. I was told this so often, by so many lesbians, that I actually began to believe it. Why, a book on dyke drama would darn near write itself. Then I actually started writing it, and suddenly *no one* wanted to talk to me.

The stigma of dyke drama was more shameful than I thought.

People I considered friends feigned sudden illness when they saw me coming. Some didn't have to feign illness—they actually *became* ill. My exes were the worst. One left this plaintive message on my voice-mail: "Please don't write about the time I threw the tofu dog at that lady's garage door..." (Five years we were together and that's all she was worried about?) Others made death threats.

Well, first my deadline was extended a few times, then it was extended indefinitely—but even when my publisher asked me to return the advance, even when after six months I was unable to provide a single chapter, I refused to quit. And it's not because I had already spent that advance on a couple of rosebushes and a stick-bug aquarium either. It's because I firmly believe in my topic.

Dyke drama is the single most important facet of lesbian culture ever!*

Everyone knows what it is, but nobody seems to know what to do about it.

This book is an attempt to know what to do about it.

Who Is This Book For?

This book is for the whining codependent martyr; for the impeccably dressed anorgasmic Hollywood lipstick lesbian; for the labrys-tattooed prison psychologist in her eighth year of sobriety; for the closeted beer-swilling softball dyke juggling several love triangles at once; for the angst-ridden, overly serious academic and her intimacy-phobic girlfriend; for the radical class-conscious batterer; for the ex still engaged in extended argumentation over formerly co-owned possessions; for the mulleted childhood hair trauma survivor; for the angry-at-the-fans-who-want-to-label-her bisexual folk singer; for the soulful paranoiac; for the fat-is-beautiful S/M dyke; for the bulimic trust-fund lesbian; and for all the other special characters in our hallowed lesbian family—and, most very especially, for all who have loved them and been loved by them, this book is for you. For those who are weary of drama, who are surrounded by drama, and who need a good cathartic cry—this book is also for you.

---

*Which is why I feel justified in fabricating so much of my research and statistics as well as embellishing history.

Reaction to This Book

"So," the girl at the Lambda fund-raiser asked, meeting my eyes as she fingered a small thread that had come loose from the sofa. "What's the title of your book?"

"It's called *Dyke Drama.*"

"Oh." [Insert blank stare. Prepare to follow the code of silence.]

"The whole title is: *Dyke Drama: Your Guide to Getting Out Alive.*"

As the formerly friendly partygoer struggled for something to say, her jaw slackened and her chin moved in a circle as if working out some kink. Clearly she was hoping she'd met the next Michael Cunningham, or some other such novelist, or at the very least a mystery writer. Her words dripped out like mildewed honey: "Sounds like that'll be a great one for the coffee table."

"Hope so." I winked, but I'd already lost her.

Her pupils snapped to the left, spotting a ficus plant she absolutely had to say hello to. Not about to let some ponytailed Book of the Month club snob disrespect my work, I went after her. She was bent, now, over the plant, squeezing a leaf as if to determine whether it was real or silk, when I grabbed her tanned, skinny arm just above its bony elbow. She turned. "Dyke d-d-drama..." I asserted, with, I admit a slight stutter (but I was angry!), "Dyke d-d-drama is no coffee table b-b-book, nor is it even c-c-close to being a coffee table subject. For your information, it's the single most important facet of lesbian culture ever!"

"I-I-I..." she began, but I wasn't finished with her yet.

"I've spent the last ten years of my graduate study on this topic!" I yelled. "I gave up studying anthropology for this topic! I gave up a Ph.D. in psychology for this topic! This is no lightweight coffee table topic!"

Dyke Drama

Well, she was immediately apologetic and admitted she was probably "just uncomfortable with the subject matter." Then she asked if I'd please release her elbow, which of course I was happy to do because I hadn't even realized I was still holding on to it, and I would never condone detaining a woman, especially another lesbian, against her will (see chapter titled "Dyke Stalkers"). After that she exuded warmth toward me again, not a full-fledged warmth like before, of course, but the kind of warmth one pretends to have for a crazy person. She smiled and patted me on the shoulder then left quickly, probably to tell others to buy my book.

Little Miss Panicked Ponytail wasn't the first to offer me negative feedback about my chosen subject matter. My own domestic partner looked nauseated when I first told her about the project, and the only progress we've made is a staunch agreement that she will not openly trash my topic anymore as long as I don't share any of the work-in-progress with her—or with any of her friends. I imagine it goes this way with all great thinkers who tackle prickly subjects such as legalized prostitution, assisted suicide, or the ethics of using stem cell research to prolong the lives of Republicans, so I don't let it bother me anymore. The truth is my reward! And now that Alyson Books has taken the bold step to ignore all common sense and publish this work, the truth can be your reward too.

Leslie Lange

What is

DYKE DRAMA?

*a brief angry history
* short definition
* long definition
* seize reality!
* river of denial
* six degrees of drama
* plot diagrams
* say hello to your inner superdyke

"What is dyke drama? Any lesbian relationship that lasts longer than one night. No, wait...any lesbian relationship that lasts long enough to require communication. No...actually, you could blindfold two dykes and put them in separate soundproof booths in separate states and still, somehow, the vibe of drama would be sparked. It's unstoppable."

—author and dyke drama survivor Michelle Sawyer

A Brief Angry History: From Sappho to The L Word

We've all heard the term *dyke drama* uttered (usually with a shrug) to explain a public spectacle we—or some of our friends—have caused, such as when Lulu storms into the local lesbian dive—eyes flashing, mouth set in a firm line, the pits of her hemp-blend Ani DiFranco T-shirt soaked—and dumps a pint of ruby mist ale in Amy's polyamorous lap. In the smoky wake of Lulu's cutely departing denimed posterior, Amy dabs herself with a cocktail napkin, rolls her eyes at the crowd, and hikes her shoulders to her ears. "Sorry," she says. "Dyke drama." And we all understand.

Who knows how the first dyke drama came about? Did God make it, or was there just a Big Bang? Sketchy records of lesbians throughout history provide little to no information, but I'll take my best stab...

Guzzlin' Greek Gals

Think back. Way back. To a time when there was neither *The L Word* nor Showtime, when there was neither Holly Near nor the Michigan Womyn's Music Festival. To a time when there wasn't even Michigan. Think back to ancient Greece. You see, the Greeks had no television, radio, or high-speed chases—that's why they invented drama. Or at least Greek drama, which is unsurprisingly the earliest precursor to what we know now in modern times as dyke drama. Then, as now, it was used as a form of entertainment. Given this fact, there's a good chance Sappho invented dyke drama. That's right, she started it. Not only was she responsible for the term *lesbian* (see the island of Lesbos, also called the "Isle of Sappho"), but she also instigated that special form of drama that surrounds wimmin who love wimmin.

The legendary poetess (circa 590 BCE) more than likely committed the first known dyke faux pas by presenting the same love poem to several different women in the same week, singing it as she strummed her lyre in front of an outdoor festival crowd one sweltering-hot summer weekend, ultimately causing a big fat Greek fracas. The chaos on Lesbos reached epic proportions. Feelings were only made worse as Greek lesbians swilled goblet after goblet of retsina, a powerful wine that tastes like floor cleaner but makes up for it by offering 100 times the buzz. Chambermaids and noblewomen alike downed 30-ounce jugs of the stuff to quell the pain of their heartsickness—and to wash down their pita bread. Soon they were so drunk they couldn't spell; they started spelling the word *women* in such crazy ways as: womon, wimmin, wymyn, womb-on, etc... This phenomenon—uncannily replicated during the 1970s feminist movement—was likely related less to women's liberation than to the fact that our earliest known ancestors—those great guzzling gals of Lesbos—were so brazenly mired in dyke drama.

Today our modern Sapphos, the Anis, OTEPs, and Pinks of the world, do their best to continue this tradition. Many, like Sappho, are short, sport silly names, and are brunette—when

their hair is not dyed neon green, that is. And many skirt the bisexual line, which always makes for more drama. Meshell Ndegeocello may be the ultimate modern Sappho, and I say this because my girlfriend believes it with all her heart and soul.

About 200 years after Sappho, another Greek lady named Philaenis (pronounced "feel anus") wrote the first illustrated lesbian sex manual, an ancient version of *The Joy of Lesbian Sex*. The book's existence fomented a small revolution (OK, so it was more like a local uproar). Who were the women depicted in the pictures? Rumors flew. Fur flew (great wads of it!). And Philaenis got ripped a new one. (Hmm, maybe I should've left Philaenis out. Oh, well—just think of her as "filler." She may have thought of herself that way.)

Centuries of Shame

Not much is known about the immediate years that followed (or preceded, for that matter), but wherever there were lots of women crammed together in small spaces, you can bet there was plenty of wild dyke drama. Medieval lesbian nuns did lots of nasty things to each other (it's a Catholic girl thing). In the courts of ancient China, when there were 3,000 women to one emperor, sexual liaisons were considered inevitable between Pekingese-toting court ladies. The Chinese used the somewhat graphic phrase *muo jingtzi,* or "rubbing mirrors," to describe lesbian sex, and the prevailing attitude was, "Hey, a little good clean friction never hurt anybody."

Enter the 20th Century

In the year 1900, a 26-year-old baby dyke named Gertrude Stein entangled herself in a lesbian love triangle with two Bryn Mawr graduates, May Bookstaver and Mabel Haynes. The drama was so thick—jealous scenes, making out under lampposts, fainting spells—that Stein dropped out of medical school and skipped the country. Thirty years later Gertrude's sweetie, Alice B. Toklas, had a cow when she found May's old love letters in the cupboard ("Whoops, forgot to tell you about that silly old love triangle, Pussy!"), and then she burned them. One can assume no match was needed. She just glared at them hard, à la *Carrie II: The Rage,* till they burst into white-hot flames. This type of drama is known as American Lesbian Expatriate Drama and has included such notables as Djuna Barnes and Hilda Doolittle.

Sufferin' for Suffragism

It has been claimed—or if it hasn't, it should be—that the entire suffragette movement was born of lesbian sexual chemistry. The bigger the mojo of the lesbian suffragette the more fervently her followers rallied to the cause. Serious lesbian Lillian Faderman has done an excellent job interpreting the romantic letters of Susan B. Anthony, but there is nothing so frank, so militant, or so explicit as the diaries of British suffragette Mary Blathwayt. According to my favorite U.K. tabloid, *The Observer,* the diaries Ms. Blathwayt kept from 1908 to 1913 reveal that "key members of the Votes for Women movement led a promiscuous lesbian lifestyle." Well, yee haw! And Ms. Blathwayt herself racked up at least ten "short-lived couplings" with various suffragettes. Her diary documents that "complicated sexual liaisons—involving the

Pankhurst family and others at the core of the militant organization—created rivalries that threatened discord." (Don't you just *love* the British?) Sounds like good old fashioned dyke drama to me.

"It does sound as if she was occasionally quite jealous," said women's suffrage expert Martin Pugh. "Christabel was the most classically beautiful of the three Pankhurst daughters and was the focus of a rash of 'crushes' across the movement." These suffragette Brits were no pacifistic hunger strikers, unlike their wimpy American counterparts. They bombed and set fire to churches, chucked bricks through winders (er, *windows*), snipped telegraph wires, and tied themselves to railings. Viewing these actions through the lens of dyke drama, it becomes hard to separate the guerrilla warfare from the jealousy-fueled tantrums. Were they all trying to outdo each other just to get into Christabel's bed? Stranger things have happened in England. (Note: American women gained equal voting rights in 1919, but their British counterparts, who were too busy tying themselves to railings and having promiscuous lesbian sex, didn't gain them until 1930. At the time, the delay seemed worth it.)

Dyke Drama's Modern Incarnations

While rich white ladies were fleeing to Paris to be lesbians, black lesbians participating in the Harlem Renaissance (1920–1935) were keepin' it real at house parties, speakeasies, drag balls, and entertainment clubs. Lesbian blues songs included Lucille Bogan's "B.D. (Bull Dyke) Woman's Blues" and Ma Rainey's "Prove It On Me." Rainey didn't back down from making lesbian allusions, including walking around in drag and posing suggestively with other women. In 1925 she was arrested when police discovered her in a room full of naked female cohorts. And they weren't changing clothes, OK?

Clandestine networks in the world of women's sports formed in the '30s, '40s, and '50s, around the same time that everyone was heading out to seedy backroom bars to meet up. These years marked our earliest sightings of "the beer-swilling loud-mouthed softball dyke." Bars were segregated, owned by the mob, and subject to frequent raids. All the tension made lesbians drink a lot. "It got so you had to choose," said Jane, an wise old lesbian I spoke with, "between the bars and your own psychological well-being."*

---

*Jane was tending the June L. Mazer Lesbian Archives in West Hollywood, Calif., when I spoke with her. See it if you have the chance, if for nothing other than the wooden labrys-shaped wall clock that hangs cockeyed over the reception desk. Go, and, for God's sake, make a donation.

These years marked the heyday of butch-femme dyke drama, when the bars teemed with heartbreaking swaggering butches, and sultry femme noirs traveled back and forth between their husbands and families and the embraces of adoring dykes. Oh, the sin!

When women weren't hanging around in bars and nightclubs, they'd curl up with a nice, juicy lesbian pulp novel. Scandalous covers. Steamy love scenes. Some lesbians saw these novels for what they were, flipping ahead to the good parts and disregarding the rest. Unfortunately, "the rest" usually involved the guilt-driven suicide of the lesbian protagonist. These books left an indelible mark on our psyches, on the one hand teaching us that we weren't alone, and on the other hand making us feel real nasty (see medieval Catholic nuns).

In the '60s things got wild and nobody is sure exactly what happened.

"A lesbian is the rage of all women condensed to the point of explosion." —Radicalesbians, 1973

The early '70s marked the birth of the "serious lesbian"—otherwise known as the "woman-identified woman"—who advocated for lesbianism as a revolutionary act. The serious lesbian had a good idea, and then just stopped having fun. She became a separatist, eschewed penetrative sex, and got really, really concerned about what everybody else was doing wrong. Not afraid to piss people off, she even tried to bully the poor straight girls: "I have had several particularly self-righteous lesbians try to pressure me—and I mean pressure me—until I was in tears, to leave my husband," wrote Leah Fritz in 1973.

Dyke Drama

Dyke drama got even more serious in the 1980s—or maybe it just made the news more often. In 1981, *Rubyfruit Jungle* author Rita Mae Brown used a handgun to blow out the rear window of Martina Navratilova's retreating

BMW, which may explain why the buff tennis great eventually came to favor the Subaru sport wagon with optional Kevlar sports bra (three feet farther from the rear window to the front seat). In the late '80s, wild-eyed Floridian Aileen Wuornos killed a handful of truckers to keep Tyria Jolene Moore in cutoff T-shirts, beer, and Ho Ho's, while on the West Coast lesbian stalker Joni Leigh Penn focused her attention on *Cagney and Lacey* costar Sharon Gless, who now plays a proud PFLAG mom on Showtime's *Queer as Folk*. Penn was no small-time stalker either. Sure, she started out small, like all stalkers, with obsessive letters and an awkward sexual pass or two, but her coup de grâce was to break into Sharon's Hollywood mansion armed with a semiautomatic rifle. What was it she planned to say that morning at 3:15 when Sharon woke cranky and bleary-eyed? "Honey, I'm home. Thought I'd just drop by tonight so we can take a nice hot bubble bath, get down, get freaky, then, who knows...perhaps engage in a cozy murder-suicide?" Whatever it was, we'll never know since—fortunately for Sharon—she was out, as in out at her boyfriend Barney's house. Barricaded inside, and with only 500 rounds of ammo, Penn held off a police SWAT team for more than seven hours before surrendering. You go, girl.

And who could ever forget poor little elfin Annie [Heche], wandering disoriented through the rural fields of Fresno while Ellen blissfully slept? She talked to space aliens. She talked to God. She went back to men. She *must* have been crazy! (I don't want to say anything against Anne Heche, though. I mean, given all that she's done for the gay community, I have to give her the benefit of the doubt. Maybe what she asked God was: "God, how can I totally rid my life of dyke drama?" And God said: "Uh, go back to men, maybe?" and God was just joking, but Anne took it seriously. Then she went on those new meds and lost her ability to dialogue one-on-one with God, and so she never found out it was just God's joke. So, Anne, if you're reading this, God told me to tell you it was all just a joke. There are lots of other ways to rid your life of dyke drama—OK, not totally, but still.)

Now it's 2005 and there's *The L Word,* an entire Showtime program dedicated to the subject of dyke drama, L.A. style. There's Shane and Marina and Francesca and Jenny and Bette and Tina and Candace and Dana and Alice. Hello? Think they'll ever run out of material? Finally a show that ignores what most lesbians look like (which I defy any one individual to define) and focuses on our daily struggle. And what struggle is that? Why, the only one we share across all religious, cultural, and racial subdivisions, of course: the struggle with our own dumb-ass behavior! And in case you haven't tuned in or noticed, there is no shortage of dumb-ass behavior portrayed on *The L Word.* Remember when Bette dry-humped the wall in that jail cell with Candace? Or when Jenny sat at the aquarium for hours with those manatees?

D-U-M-B A-S-S

So the next time you hear some armchair TV critic lamenting the absence of lesbian looks we're used to *seeing,* remind her that

HOW DO YOU DEFINE DYKE DRAMA?

"Um, drama that involves dykes?" —Stacy L.

"Dyke drama is the overblown, out of proportion, inappropriate way gay women react to each other's comments and actions (no matter how insignificant) once they've slept together." —anonymous

"The constant soap opera many of us immerse ourselves in, which often is a result of lesbian lovers' circles we create because our best friends are our exes." —Mia D.

"An emotional entanglement that gets complex and melodramatic because two women can't tell they may love each other but don't need to be together so they're always trying to hold on." —lesbian author Jewelle Gomez

"Dyke drama in general is the kind of overly thought-out worldview that seems to accompany a woman's discovery that she likes other women. The same way that when guys come

out a vast majority develop lisps and affect a sincere affection for Astroglide and house music, dyke drama is a kind of inherited hysteria that demands that I adore k.d. lang and care A LOT about identity politics." —Bridget C.

"Dyke drama is what happens when you meet someone hot at a bar in a city you've never visited and in which you know no one, make arrangements to get coffee the next day, and, while having an actual conversation, while sober, discover that she is the most recent ex of your first girlfriend and knows stuff about you even you had forgotten—like that thing about the Dr. Bronner's Peppermint Soap." —J.D.

"Dyke drama is the narrative enacted by lesbian codependents engaged in extended argumentation—often with the involvement of their respective support groups/systems— about issues of fidelity, control, or other relational issues, which may or may not be sexual." —Shelly

"Lesbians behaving like junior high school kids." —J.B.

what she *is* getting is a bird's-eye view, from the safety of her own beanbag chair, of all the feelings and dilemmas we're used to *processing*. *The L Word* is the show that says simultaneously: "Here is what we do" (insert scene with tits and ass) and "Here is what not to do" (insert next scene with tits and ass rubbing up against another set of tits and ass), all while serving up those moments of dignity, friendship, hope, and true love that exist between the lines, plus a steady stream of excellent cinematography—for soft porn, that is. This is true progress.

A Short Definition

If dyke drama were ever to take its rightful place in Webster's Dictionary, the definition might read:

1: a behavior or dynamic related to stereotypical qualities of lesbians taken to such an extreme that it serves to entertain the community as a whole 2: lesbian interactions that do not serve the good of the individual, the lesbian community, or the general populace—as in the case of premature cohabitation, lesbian bed death, and other unpleasant phenomena.

Let's break this ugly beast down to its two root words:

drama: a situation or succession of events in real life having the dramatic progression or emotional content characteristic of a play

and

dyke 1: common slang for "lesbian" 2: a lesbian who's a little rough around the edges (Nothing wrong with that, of course! She's just a little...rough.)

Leslie Lange

"Dyke drama," therefore, is simply when lesbians find themselves in a situation that has the dramatic progression or emotional content characteristic of a play. What type of play? Why, any type of play! From *A Comedy of Errors* to *Death of a Salesman*. However, it would be a mistake to put too much emphasis on the part about plays—I mean, the difference is obvious: One is real; one is make-believe. Lesbians who try to make themselves feel better by repeating the mantra "This is not real. This is only a play" will be well served by paying attention to the "real-life" part of the above definition, because this author is here to tell the unsugarcoated truth: Dyke drama may be entertaining, but a play it is not. It's as real as Phranc's flattop, so burp-seal your Tupperware and get used to it.

But still, the definitions put forth are lacking...something. What? Perhaps the intangible: a screwball, primal, hormonal force that can never be tamed, let alone named, and this is why we shrug it off as a mystery, or a joke, or just, well, dumb.

Based on my minimal and biased research, I would like to suggest a long definition of dyke drama, apt because most dyke drama goes on for a long time—and also apt because I don't want to miss anything. We all know how pissed lesbians get when they feel misrepresented. What if I, who only just recently bribed my way *off* a major lesbian blacklist in the Pacific Northwest, haven't done enough research? What if I get it wrong? Or worse, what if I haven't done enough processing? Anyway, at the risk of over-processing...

A Long Definition

Dyke drama is a true-life succession of events that contains one or more of the following elements:

• a convoluted backstory (a.k.a. "the lesbian tale of woe")

"Drama is part of romance, that's for sure. We all crave emotional moments, surprises, deeply felt passions, and even a sort of gentle possessiveness. But dyke drama sets itself apart from ordinary drama by drawing in extended networks of participants to witness and sometimes share in this emotionalism gone wildly out of control." —Shelly

---

- premature cohabitation (two women move in together within less than two heartbeats of their first kiss)

- a protracted unacknowledged romance in which neither woman will admit an attraction for the other (see lesbian romance novels)

- in the event of a romantic separation, continuing to share an apartment or home for a length of time that is deemed ridiculous by anyone's standards (a.k.a. "lez be friends")

- cat (or other pet) upkeep, custody, or allergy issues

- the expiration of sexuality between two partners (lesbian bed death)

- victim status sought by both parties

Leslie Lange

- infidelity stemming from a lesbian-only social event such as a potluck, barbeque, barbeque-potluck, folk music festival, moonlit hike, Olivia cruise, girls' night out at the club, prison yard recreation hour, or Dinah Shore Weekend

- lengthy dialogue in which subjects are discussed over and over and the focus on feelings leads to one or both parties wallowing in them. This is often called "processing," as it renders the brain stem's consistency to that of processed ham

- simultaneous PMS (among two or more women) and its uglier twin: simultaneous menopause

- the involvement of an extended network of ex-lovers, usually referred to as "a lesbian's best friends"

- an overblown, out-of-proportion reaction to all that is said and done, sometimes manifested as a lack of sense of humor or other healthy coping mechanisms

- the existence of blacklists, by means of which taboo breakers or code violators are systematically shunned by a particular lesbian clique

Dyke drama also has a wide range of definitions and classifications within itself. For example:

Petty dyke drama involves gossiping and complaining to your friends, throwing tantrums, minor acts of betrayal, and generally bad manners or classless behavior.

Moderate dyke drama includes infidelity, sex triangles, group snubs, threats (such as to out someone to coworkers or parents), and secretive stalking.

18

Serious dyke drama involves physical violence, public spectacle, self-mutilation, open stalking, threats made or carried out with firearms, calls to the police, kid- or pet-napping, and hired hit men/women.

All forms of dyke drama, however, are exacerbated by the underlying frustrations of being a second-class citizen times two: the isolation of the closet, the toll of self-hatred, the social and economic disadvantages of being both a woman and gay. Is it possible that we project our anger at the world onto our partner? Onto our community as a whole? When all is said and done, dykes who have fully integrated their lives with straight and gay friends and family are much less likely to dwell in the muck of dyke drama.

Seize Reality!

Show me a lesbian who says she hasn't been affected by dyke drama and I'll show you a damn liar. My informal survey of personal ads on PlanetOut.com revealed the following: Second only to "I enjoy long walks on the beach..." the phrase that popped up most often was "not into drama" or its more specific variant "not into dyke drama."

Who do we think we're kidding? Lesbians taking pains to distance themselves from dyke drama are likely to have already struggled through their fair share. To test this theory, I posted an airbrushed photo and doctored profile of myself on PlanetOut and procured dates with five random interested women who had professed not to be into dyke drama in their personal ads. The result of this uncontrolled experiment were disturbing: Five out of five women claiming to be tired of dyke drama spent the majority of their dates dwelling on it.

Date number 1, Carrie, talked about how her ex-girlfriend, Rita, had developed a crush on another woman. Date number 2, Tracy,

had just gotten out of the hospital with a dislocated shoulder, suffered when a member of the U.S. Women's Field Hockey team broke down her door after she spotted Tracy fondling her girlfriend's breasts in a public park. Date number 3 had her dog kidnapped by a private investigator hired by her lover of 13 years. Date number 4 had received the "silent treatment" from other lesbians in her social circle because, as she put it, "None of them could understand my special capacity—a gift, really, is how I consider it—to love more than one woman at the same time." Date number 5, a kindly woman with dark circles under her eyes, had attended a Kaiser Permanente-sponsored support group for partners of people diagnosed with cancer, then found out the "medication" her lover was on was actually heroin.

Dyke Drama

River of Denial

A lesbian, stuck in a flimsy rubber raft, is faced with an oncoming frothy stretch of rapids. Which self-statement gives her a better chance of survival?

a. "I'm not into rapids, and besides, this life vest isn't made of all-natural biodegradable products, so screw it! I'll just close my eyes and pretend it's not happening."

b. "Holy shit! A-a-ah!" (flail, flail, flail)

c. "Holy shit! But, hey, I am on a friggin' *river* after all. And I *did* get in the boat. Where's my paddle? Now, what did that river guide say I was supposed to do with it?"

The point is, we've all got to grow up and, for Pete's sake, start paddling! Denying that dyke drama exists, especially while immersed in it, can be hazardous: You could wind up walking home in the rain without an umbrella, for example. Or an angrily packed and hurled-out-the-window duffel bag could land on your head, causing permanent short-term memory loss. Wall-punching, I'll have you know, is the leading cause of lesbian fifth-metacarpal fractures.

But in the face of these horrifying examples—and I've obviously toned them down some!—don't lose heart, girls. Why? Because there's hope. Yes, really. There truly is hope. You just have to choose option "c." You have to acknowledge the river. What to do with the paddle, how to get yourself through those dark swirling eddies and sharp, blood-spattered rocks, well, that's something you can learn from a professional instructor, someone who's taken the time to research and practice, who's been sucked into some of those eddies and who's hit her head on some of those jagged rocks. People like me—a gal with some lumps.

Six Degrees of Drama

Before we get to the hows and wherefores of navigating dyke drama, it's first necessary to come to understand it better, to establish a framework by which we can judge the severity of your drama and the amount of effort needed to get through it. Just like river rapids, dyke drama can be broken into six primary classifications:

Class One: Mild Drama (Beginner)

These are common everyday sorts of things that happen to all lesbians. Dyke feathers get ruffled. A sharp verbal exchange is witnessed by others. A woman storms out of a public gathering, such as a party or dinner, over a seemingly trivial issue.

Class Two: Entertaining Drama (Histrionic)

Class II drama occurs when someone makes a really big deal out of nothing. For example: A harmless object, such as a Boca Burger, is thrown at another object, such as a lamp, with the result being that someone is coerced into attending anger management classes. Or, a woman who is asked out on a date imagines she is being stalked.

Class Three: Moderate Drama (Classic)

This usually involves multiple twists and turns with a shocking element of surprise or two. Details are hashed over repeatedly by all parties involved. Resistance to return to normalcy is high. The incident spreads as folklore throughout the lesbian community in an individual city or county. A gay male friend may be asked to arbitrate. Example: a breakup that involves deception with a third party, with lots of phone calls, ranting e-mails, and processing stirred in.

Class Four: High Drama (Expert)

High drama involves multiple occurrences of severe drama and includes but is not limited to: threats (including suicide threats), acts of revenge, custody battles (children and pets), or damage to property. Sharp or just really heavy objects, such as knives, bowling balls, and marble figurines, may be thrown or wielded. Three or more of the five natural disasters of lesbian sex are usually present: drunkenness, fire, absurd formation of emotional attachment, lopsided three-way (in which two women are way more into each other than they are into the third), and sexually transmitted disease.

Class Five: Extreme Drama

Extreme drama always involves newsworthy public spectacle and includes all drama that leads to real (not just perceived) personal injury or a minimum of 24 hours of institutionalization in a psych unit, prison ward, or suspected-terrorist holding tank. Other components include: self-mutilation, suicide attempts, break-ins, brandished firearms, physical violence, and communications with God (beyond ordinary prayer) or alien space visitors (beyond belonging to a *Star Trek* fan club). Criminal activity is often a prevalent ingredient.

Class Six: Off the Charts

This type of drama includes criminal activity and violence combined with a high probability of loss of life. Class VI dyke drama is defined as dangerous for any lesbian, regardless of experience, and is generally only for those with little or no sense of self-preservation. Usually involves the arrival of police, SWAT teams, and news helicopters. My recommendation: RUN FOR YOUR LIFE!

-----------------------------✍🏻-----------------------------

True Testimonial:
One Lesbian's Soul-Searching and Poignant Portrayal of Her Experiences With Drama

"Because women tend to be more compassionate, more able to listen, and more interested in taking care of others, it becomes more difficult to just break up, stay apart, and not get all ensnared by emotion. I also liken the experience to a phenomenon I encountered while working at a women's bookstore. We were the only women's bookstore in a major city, serving the community in all sorts of ways: as a meeting place, as a source of literature by and about women you could not get anywhere else, etc. Still, women would come in and redress us for the smallest things.

'You don't carry XXXL T-shirts, and I find that to be really offensive to large women.'

'Your CDs are priced too high.'

'Such and such a book should be shelved differently.'

On and on.

I had worked in a general bookstore and never encountered so much whining to the management. Staff in the women's bookstore worked so hard and for so little pay to provide all members of the women's community all they could not find elsewhere, and still we were constantly harangued by dissatisfied women. I came to believe that women feel more able to complain to other women. We are so afraid of confronting men or heterosexuals, or the mainstream, that we save all of our gripes and expectations for each other. I think some lesbians treat their female partners similarly. We are more able to confront women, to ask them for what we need, and to rebel against them. We're still afraid of 'the man.' In that way, lesbian relationships can be all

Dyke Drama

stretched out by drama, and at times emotional manipulation, that I don't think occurs as much between men and women.

But I think the root of this problem is good: We can communicate with each other more easily than perhaps any other combination of companions. And there is power in that—we just have to work hard at not taking advantage of our partners' compassion." —Debbie R.

What Does Dyke Drama Look Like?

Very little dyke drama follows the traditional dramatic progression of a linear plot, with the introduction of a **conflict** or problem, a **series of escalations** that leads to the **climax,** and a **denouement** (long French word meaning "the end").

The primary difference between most dyke drama and classic drama is that in classic drama the heroine learns something and accomplishes her goals. In dyke drama this happens only occasionally (OK, almost never), and when it does we call it the **shift phenomenon.** The shift phenomenon occurs when dyke drama leads to a classic-drama outcome. This is called emotional evolution and is one of the secrets to "getting out alive."

The basic structure of a lot of dyke drama is perhaps best represented by Stephen Karpman's drama triangle, which involves a victim, rescuer, and persecutor.

In this configuration, the "victim" partner is rescued from hairy situations by the "rescuer" partner. When and if the rescuer partner refuses to rescue the victim partner, the victim partner sees the rescuer as her "persecutor." Generally, this dynamic occurs throughout the duration of the relationship—and often well into the breakup.

The case of Teresa M. is a perfect example of the triangular victim-rescuer-persecutor dynamic. It all started when Teresa's lover broke things off with her while she was in possession of Teresa's car, "my beloved '69 Karmann Ghia that I gamely lent her when her own boring Honda Civic was stolen." Teresa had her motorcycle to get around on, and since her lover had observed on more than one occasion that Teresa often wasn't there for her in the way she needed her to be, giving her the car seemed like the right thing to do.

"She broke up with me on my answering machine the following day, something about feeling crowded by me and needing her space at this 'difficult' time," Teresa told me. "She didn't even mention the car."

Storm clouds rolled into town, and Teresa spent the next five days getting soaked as she took her motorcycle to and from work and school. She was too proud to call her ex, and she figured the woman needed the car more than she did anyway. On the fifth day, the ex called to say she was sorry she had blamed Teresa for her problems and invited her back in from the cold. After some requisite kissing and making up, Teresa told her lover she could keep the car as long as she needed it, to which her lover replied that she didn't need it, actually, that her mother had been out of the country and she had use of her SUV in the meantime. In fact, she said, it had been really difficult parking both vehicles in her crowded neighborhood for the past several days.

"I should have broken up with her on the spot," Teresa lamented, "but, to my eternal shame, I did not."

In Teresa's case, her lover was the "victim" while Teresa was the "rescuer" and also the "persecutor." The dyke drama unfolded from there.

The drama triangle has its exits, but they aren't always visible. When trapped in a burning building, people often crowd and trample each other to get to the "only" available exit stairwell. Their hysteria hinders them from seeing that there is a perfectly accessible alternative stairwell nearby.

Queer scholar Justine Moss has suggested the "circle of hysteria" to describe a pattern characterized by movement of a single point of contention that orbits from escalation to escalation to escalation, creating a vortex of emotion that sucks in all who come near it. Moss calls this circle "The Big O" of dyke drama, alluding to the almost sexualized frenzy of participation en route to the ultimate goal: senseless chaos.

Because Moss's circle is in continuous escalation, there is no feasible exit once a subject is sucked in. The only possible climax is the implosion of both personal and communal space.

Dissatisfied with both the triangle and the circle, some fellow scholars and I consulted a couple of old statistics and physics textbooks (50 cents at a garage sale, such a steal!) and sat down with them for an afternoon as we shared a six-pack of beer. Although I am unable to replicate our work, I am more than happy to share our conclusions. The complex and constantly undulating structure of the purest forms of dyke drama can be diagrammed only as a traversing and reversing, multidirectional scribble that resembles the typical wad of pubic hair in a plugged shower drain at your local municipal pool.

But whatever dyke drama looks like, our most shameful secrets are contained in it. It's the garbage bin of our psyches, the dirty diaper we toddle around in. Just remember that, as we are shamed, so we are defined. Our conflicts and struggles are our deepest truths!

Say Hello to Your Inner SuperDyke

Whatever the structure of the drama, when you're a dyke you'll have to deal with it. I once had a lover with an addiction problem about whom her sister said, "Loren is like a cat. No matter what kind of mess she gets into, she always lands on her feet." Well, most of us are not Loren. Tragically, most of us land on our asses (and, well, not so tragically, most of us are not on crack). But we can learn to do it too—not crack, of course (which anyone can learn), but to always land catlike on perfectly prepared little paws.

Any motivated lesbian can learn to navigate, enjoy, or just plain neutralize dyke drama simply by reinventing herself as a form of superhero, a modern SuperDyke—a "Super Sappho" if you will. Faster than a speeding mullet! Able to leap lesbian tall tales in a single bound. She's not a crime fighter; she's a drama fighter, with the capacity to see it coming from miles and miles away, armed with X-ray vision to see into the hearts of really scary sociopaths. The Super Sappho is a fearless tamer of wild she-devils, cracking her magic bullwhip at the gnarliest one of all: that long-fanged roaring hellcat within.

And you, my Sapphic sisters, you can do this too.

No, really. I mean it.

And if you find that you can't tame the dyke drama in your life, that's OK too. No one's here to judge anybody else, OK? This book is intended to be a safe space—a "safe house"—where any and all things are cool, even the most pathetic and miserable forms of failure and character defect. Remember, there is an upside to dyke drama. Just give me a moment to think of what that might be...oh, yes! Other lesbians will use you as an example of exactly how *not* to do things. We'll all learn from your mistakes. As tales of your ridiculous exploits travel by word of mouth, you will be improving the quality of other lesbian lives. But mostly, other lesbians will appreciate your gift to the community in the form of nonstop quality entertainment. What could be more rewarding than that?

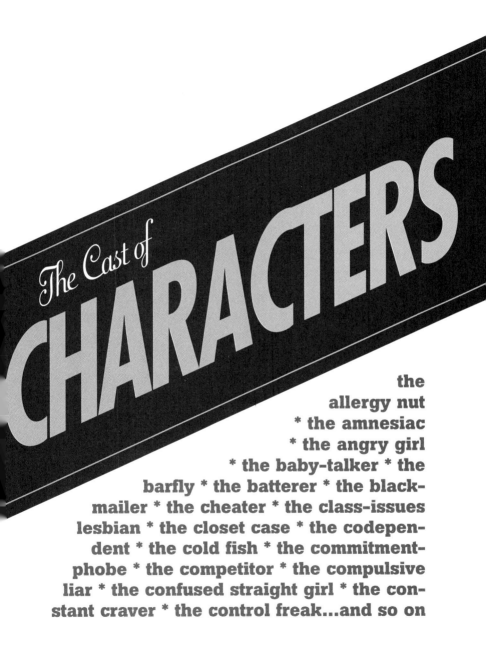

The Cast of **CHARACTERS**

the allergy nut * the amnesiac * the angry girl * the baby-talker * the barfly * the batterer * the blackmailer * the cheater * the class-issues lesbian * the closet case * the codependent * the cold fish * the commitmentphobe * the competitor * the compulsive liar * the confused straight girl * the constant craver * the control freak...and so on

"She had really annoying personality quirks. But we're still long-distance pals." —Beverly

In all drama, there are roles to play, but in dyke drama, they're just a little more special. The following is an attempt to list some of the prominent players, to capture the essence of their strategies, their voices, what it is about them that represents the central nature of lesbian troublemaking. Keep in mind that these are merely approximations of the most basic bad behaviors. Dangerous, manipulative, and aggravating mutations continue to surface in both urban and rural areas.

Disclaimer: You may currently be involved with a woman who resembles one or more of these characters. You may currently resemble one or more of these characters yourself. You may have several exes who resemble these characters. You may be the ex of several women because you epitomize one or more of these characters. However, while any or all of the above statements may apply to you, they are in no way based on you specifically—or your life. OK?*

*Even if you know, or have slept with, Leslie Lange.

The Allergy Nut: She's allergic to everything, including your mohair sweater, your perfume, your dog, the lawn, and maybe even you. **Pros:** You'll be one of the few people who understand the difference between Flonase and Claritin. **Cons:** She may claim she's allergic to sex. **Often heard line:** "Can you open a window?"

The Amnesiac: She claims you never told her things, rewrites history, denies bad behavior she admitted to before, etc. **Pros:** Spend $70 on a digital voice recorder and your worries are over. **Cons:** You're a lesbian, right? $70 is way over your budget. **Often heard line:** "Huh?"

The Angry Girl: Anger, from time to time, is a healthy emotion, but this chick has no sense of reality. She'll scream obscenities and break things at the drop of a tofu block. **Pros:** Always exciting if you like a little spice. **Cons:** Extreme anger is a gateway to other forms of abuse. **Often heard line:** "Why I oughta…"

The Baby-Talker: Her larynx is stuck on a single squeezed-out note. She goos. She gahs. She may even use a pacifier. **Pros:** If your breasts like a lot of attention, she'll bring out the nurturer in you. **Cons:** Embarrassing in public places. **Often heard line:** "Ma-ma!"

The Barfly: She loves hanging out at the local lesbian watering hole. Every time you go out, she'll insist you go to a bar. **Pros:** She'll never remember any wrongdoing on your part. **Cons:** She'll never remember any wrongdoing on *her* part. **Often heard line:** "It's 2-for-1 well drinks at Attitudes."

The Batterer: This is serious stuff and happens more than many might think in lesbian relationships. If someone is physically assaulting you, get out of the relationship IMMEDIATELY. **Pros:** What doesn't kill you makes you stronger. **Cons:** The pro applies only after you've left her. **Often heard lie:** "It won't happen again."

The Blackmailer: Try to break up with her and she'll threaten to out you to your entire family and neighborhood and all your coworkers. **Pros:** She doesn't mind if you're in the closet—it gives her more power. **Cons:** Do you always want to feel like you're teetering on the edge of a cliff? **Often heard line:** "Gee, I wonder what your boss would think of this photo..."

The Cheater: She'll lie. She'll sleep around. She'll play you like a fool. **Pros:** You'll feel less guilty if you're a cheater too. **Cons:** The presence of human papillomavirus is the leading cause of cervical cancer. **Often heard line:** "I've gotta work late, hon."

The Class-Issues Lesbian: Everything is reduced to class. Fancy restaurants are too "bourgeois." Brand names are "elitist." You're a snob if you own a car. Any criticism of her stems from your inability to appreciate the fact that she grew up on a Mississippi pig farm. **Pros:** You'll become more socially conscious. **Cons:** Whatever happened to having fun? **Often heard line:** "How can you be sure that wasn't made in a sweatshop?"

The Closet Case: We've all been in the closet at some point, but when she's 35, lives in the Castro, and works for a lesbian-owned construction company, isn't enough enough? Who does she think she's fooling? **Pros:** You'll spend a lot of cozy time at home together with the curtains drawn. **Cons:** You'll never get to go to an Indigo Girls concert. (Wait, maybe that's a pro!) **Often heard line:** "People from work might be there."

The Codependent: You need her for your dysfunctional relationship. She needs you for her dysfunctional relationship. **Pros:** She'll always be there for you. **Cons:** She'll always be there for you. **Often heard line:** "You need me just as much as I need you."

The Cold Fish: She acts like she's a sex freak, but when you get her in bed she just lies there. **Pros:** Great, if you're just a cuddler. **Cons:** Obvious. **Often heard line:** "Just give me a minute."

The Commitmentphobe: For her, five years is too soon to think about living together. **Pros:** You'll have lots of alone time. **Cons:** You'll constantly wonder if there's something wrong with you. **Often heard line:** "Just wait till I'm settled in my career."

The Competitor: This may be something minor, as in scattering the tiles when she doesn't win at Scrabble. Or it may be something major, as in being insanely competitive with you in terms of career, accomplishments, and friends. **Pros:** You'll gain insight into why ex–figure skater Tonya Harding hired a thug to maim Nancy Kerrigan. **Cons:** You may openly gloat when she loses—and wind up not really liking yourself very much anymore. **Often heard line:** "You got up at 6? I got up at 5."

The Compulsive Liar: Always has an alibi, even when she doesn't need one. Gets a crazy high from spinning outrageous yarns. Tries to impress others with a long list of bogus accomplishments and tribulations. **Pros:** Will lie for you in court. **Cons:** You'll never really know her. **Often heard line:** "As I dragged three bodies from the collapsing World Trade Center..."

----------------------------✍🏻----------------------------
True Testimonial:
One Lesbian's Adventure With a Compulsive Liar

"I met 'Becky' at the French Quarter restaurant in West Hollywood, where I regularly waited on the post-meeting gatherings of myriad 12-step groups she attended. Depending on the day of the week, Becky was likely to show up with Alcoholics

Anonymous, Narcotics Anonymous, Overeaters Anonymous, or Codependents Anonymous—a level of issue-mongering I might better have avoided. A charismatic storyteller, Becky was often called upon to speak at 12-step meetings, making her a natural leader among the addicted. For my own susceptibility I blame the vice of drama, the narrative kind.

One moment I was her waitress, casually commenting that I liked her newly shaved head, and before I could catch myself I had entered her realm, giving her rides to UCLA for fake oncology appointments. Apparently her treatment was going very well; her fake cancer was in full remission. It was bone cancer, actually, complete with a self-inflicted 'surgical' scar on her right calf.

But there was a lot more to Becky than just fake cancer; she was—or, more properly, was not—also a former concert violinist, a child prodigy who took to European concert stages at the age of eight. But long symphony tours during her teenage years eventually took their toll as she turned to booze and pills to quell her loneliness and anxiety; she became addicted to a variety of substances, all of which would eventually not kill her and therefore make her stronger. Before she could triumph, however, she had to fall farther yet. Her career in shambles by her late teens, drug-addled Becky was sent home to her parents only to be kicked out of the house. It was during a stay at a gay and lesbian youth shelter that she discovered her true sexuality. (In her fake back story, she faked a homosexual identity in order to stay at the center, but then she realized she actually was a lesbian—but maybe not really since it was a fake story. No one knows for sure.)

Becky's 40th birthday was approaching, and her closest friends, many of whom had known her for the better part of a decade, hit on the idea of throwing her a This Is Your Life party. They tracked down Becky's mother and sister in hopes of enlisting their help to contact some of the notable figures from her past. The façade Becky had maintained for years was shattered instantly. To the chagrin of dozens of people she had sponsored through 12-step programs, she had no known problems with drugs or alcohol. Becky had never traveled outside the United States, nor had she ever been homeless. She had never played the violin. Her only prodigious talent was for lying. And there was, of course, no cancer. I never saw her again. Becky spent her birthday in police custody, charged with felony fraud by a friend who had supported her through

Dyke Drama

eight months of fake disability and flown her to Lourdes after she expressed interest in the healing waters of Saint Bernadette's grotto.

I was working a shift at the restaurant one night when her friends pulled me aside to debrief me. They wanted to know what the nature of our relationship had been and whether we had ever been sexual with one another. 'We were friends,' I told them. 'Nothing more.' There was never a kiss; we never made love. She told me stories. She read to me from a fake novel she had not written. They wanted to know how I felt about all of this—the manipulation, the fraud, the lies she told about me, about me with her. I told them I was sorry she wasn't real, that I felt like a friend had died, and that I would miss her. I still do." —Teresa M.

---------------------------❦---------------------------

The Confused Straight Girl: She's like a teeter-totter: One minute she's in love with you, the next she's back with her boyfriend. She may even invite you to have a ménage à trois. **Pros:** Seducing a straight girl is always a thrill. **Cons:** You'll be dragged through the mire of her sexual confusion. **Often heard line:** "Wanna come over and watch a movie?"

The Constant Craver: She thinks the lyrics to k.d. lang songs are gospel. Whenever you go over to her place, she's got k.d. on the stereo. Yep, she's pretty much in love with her. (Other variants: the Melissa Etheridge Maniac and the Ellen DeGeneres Joke-Quoter.) **Pros:** You won't have to spend a lot of money buying CDs for her because she already has all she wants. **Cons:** How many times can you listen to "Big Boned Gal"? **Often heard line:** "If you just cut your hair and put on a vest..."

The Control Freak: She tells you what to wear. She orders for you at restaurants. In extreme cases she won't let you leave the house without her permission. **Pros:** Your mind will always feel rested. **Cons:** Your mind will atrophy and you'll have no life. **Often heard line:** "Where do you think you're going?"

The Couples Therapy Addict: If you've been in couples therapy for more than a year, this is you, or your girlfriend. **Pros:** A little enlightenment is always a good thing. **Cons:** If you need a third party to fix your day-to-day problems after this much time, you might as well break up. You know it's really bad when you have to start selling things to pay for your weekly sessions. **Often heard line:** "Hurry up, we're going to be late."

The Crazy Ex: Oy, oy, oy. What more can I say, except she is without a doubt the most volatile player in the dyke drama. She may even encompass five or ten dyke-drama cast members, including the Smear Campaigner, the Stalker, the Drama Addict, the "No Boundaries" Freak, and the Manipulator, to name a few. Word of advice: Try as hard as you can to take yourself out of the equation. **Pros:** If you're addicted to drama, you don't need to lift a finger. **Cons:** Court costs, psychological trauma, the hassle of filing restraining orders...it all gets old pretty fast. **Often heard line:** "If only you knew the real me..."

The Crybaby: You change the TV channel, she cries. You tell her you'll call her back at 9 and you call at 9:03, she cries. Anything doesn't go her way, she cries. If you cry, she cries even harder. **Pros:** She's in touch with her feelings—well, at least one of them. **Cons:** High Kleenex bills. **Often heard line:** "You don't love me."

The Date Breaker: She'll call you an hour before your date with some lame excuse about her mother being rushed to the hospital, her car breaking down, etc. **Pros:** If you don't have

much energy, it can be a good thing. **Cons:** You'll be like Whoopi Goldberg munching on breadsticks waiting for her date in *Jumpin' Jack Flash*. **Often heard line:** "My puppy just swallowed a Nexium and I've got to take her to the emergency room."

Denial Girl: She's broke, but she lives off her credit cards. You've told her it's over, but she acts like you're still together. You've only been on two dates and she's telling people you're her girlfriend. Whatever the truth is, it's reversed in her mind. No, she's not the crazy one—you are! **Pros:** She'll buy you expensive gifts even though she can't pay her electric bill. **Cons:** Once she starts acting like you owe her something, those gifts will have to be returned. **Often heard line:** "Yeah, right."

The Drama Addict: This girl really needs it. Dyke drama makes her tick. If she's not harassing her ex, maxing out your credit cards, or keeping tabs on you 24/7, she's not happy—in fact, she's bored. **Pros:** Life is never boring. **Cons:** Life should be peaceful and full of joy. **Often heard line:** "I hacked into your computer last night..."

The Drug Abuser: She's addicted to a controlled substance and needs to have it to function on a daily basis, or she may not be addicted to drugs but needs to take them to have a good time. **Pros:** None. **Cons:** She may be abusive, have mood swings, or require serious medical attention. She may also drain your bank account or steal your stuff and sell it in order to get her next fix. **Often heard line:** "I didn't go to work today."

The Drunk: She may be a full-blown alcoholic or a weekend warrior. **Pros:** She's the life of the party. **Cons:** She's the life of the party until she starts (a) bawling; (b) vomiting; (c) wrecking your ca; (d) hitting on someone else's girlfriend; or (e) throwing punches at you. **Often heard line:** "I'll go to a meeting. I really mean it this time."

The Erotica Junkie: She doesn't want to have sex because she gets all she needs from erotica books, online porn, and videos. **Pros:** You'll have a candy store at your fingertips. **Cons:** You won't have *her* at your fingertips. **Often heard line:** "I'm going to the store."

The Ex-Obsesser: On your first date, she'll mention her ex several times. On your second date, she'll give you details of the horrible breakup. On your third date, you'll just happen to go to the restaurant where the ex works. It's a downward spiral from there. **Pros:** Perfect for those who wish to avoid intimacy. **Cons:**

You'll always be second fiddle. **Often heard line:** "I'm going out for a drive." (i.e., a drive-by!)

The Extreme Social Activist: She spends all of her time helping the homeless, sponsoring alcoholics, or volunteering at the animal shelter, but when you have a problem or need a shoulder to cry on, she's unavailable. **Pros:** It's very inspiring being around people who want to make a difference in the world. **Cons:** She's changing the world, but she's never heard the phrase "Think globally, act locally"—locally meaning you! **Often heard line:** "I'm booked Wednesday night. How about three weeks from Thursday?"

The Extreme Sports Fanatic: She can't be there for the birth of your child? Can you blame her? It's the WNBA play-offs, for cryin' out loud! **Pros:** Sports fans on average take better care of their bodies. **Cons:** Then there are those who use sporting events as an excuse to wash down a dozen glazed Krispy Kreme doughnuts with a six-pack of frosty Miller Genuine Draft. **Often heard line:** "Just a few more minutes. It's sudden-death overtime!"

The Fixer: She's got a solution for everything and has no problem telling you what it is. She may also try to fix your problems behind your back by talking to your friends, your ex, your family, etc. **Pros:** If you're lazy or stupid, she may be able to help you out. **Cons:** You'll lose your independence, your sense of self, and your decision-making abilities. **Often heard line:** "What's your therapist's number?"

The Fix-It-Upper: She's too busy doing home repairs to spend time with you. There may not even be any home repairs to make, but she'll always find something. **Pros:** Watching a woman spackle can be kinda sexy. **Cons:** You may end up with a spiral staircase that leads to nowhere. **Often heard line:** "Anybody seen my drill bit?"

The Flirt: You go out to dinner and she flirts with the waitress. She's always telling the bartender how pretty she is. She may even massage her female friends in public (see "The Public Massager"). **Pros:** Isn't that how you met her in the first place? **Cons:** Say hello to your brand new, completely modernized inferiority complex! **Often heard line** (not said to you): "Your eyes are like magic."

The Foreign Objects Freak: She's obsessed with putting all kinds of weird objects into your hoo-hoo during sex (bananas, wine bottles, zucchini, her grandmother's cane...). **Pros:** If that's your thing... **Cons:** Could damage your thing. **Often heard line:** "Call 911!"

The $14 Lesbian: She'll make you pay for everything because she always claims she only has $14 in her checking account. This claim may or may not be true. **Pros:** You'll always feel generous around her. **Cons:** Pretty soon *you'll* only have $14 in your checking account. **Often heard line:** "There's a three-day hold on my paycheck."

The Gay Male Intervener: He will try to mediate between you and your girlfriend. He will beg you both to end the drama. **Pros:** It's always good to have some outside perspective. **Cons:** You may not like it when he minimizes your feelings. Plus, the little busybody may escalate the drama by playing "she said, she said." **Often heard line:** "Girlfriend, stop!"

The Germophobe: She takes her own food to restaurants, brings Clorox wipes on overnight trips, and compulsively microwaves the dish sponge. **Pros:** Just relax and let her do all the worrying about salmonella and botulism. **Cons:** You may start to feel dirty—or worse, germy. You may even start to feel germy after a shower. **Often heard line:** "You washed your hands (with antibacterial liquid soap) after you touched that, right?"

The Girl with One Excuse After Another (see also "The Date Breaker"): She's supposed to pick up the dry cleaning, but she had a late business meeting. The rent is due, but she had an "unexpected expense." You're languishing in bed with the flu, but she couldn't pick up your medicine because she had a flat tire. **Pros:** You'll be more self-sufficient than ever. **Cons:** She's completely unreliable and will make you never want to trust another woman again. **Often heard line:** "My alarm clock didn't go off."

The Googler: On your first date, she knows everything about you because she looked you up on the Internet. She may also have purchased a background check. **Pros:** You won't have to say much, because she already knows everything about you. **Cons:** She's way creepy. **Often heard line:** "So, you played softball in 1993..."

The Group Dater: She will only go out on dates with other couples or as part of a larger group. **Pros:** If you're not into her, you'll have plenty of gals to choose from. **Cons:** You won't have any private time, and you won't feel very special. **Often heard line:** "It's Women on a Roll's moonlit basket-weaving night. Wanna come?"

The Gym Freak: She spends all her time working out. **Pros:** She'll have a hot body. **Cons:** She'll be obsessed with her body and may judge *your* unhealthy diet and lack of exercise. **Often heard line:** "I'll skip the bread, thanks."

The Hypocrite: She says she's a vegan but secretly eats Whoppers. She claims she's a member of the Green Party, but she voted for Bush. She gives long speeches about respecting Mother Nature but was spotted tossing a cigarette butt out of her Range Rover. **Pros:** If you're just into appearances, then you've found the right woman. **Cons:** Your word is the most important thing you own. **Often heard line:** "I could never date someone who pretended to be someone other than who she is."

The Inner-Child Addict: All her problems stem from the fact that her single mother worked nights and she had to take care of 12 siblings. If you have a problem, she tells you to sit down and "dialogue" with your inner child. **Pros:** You may discover some revealing insights about yourself. **Cons:** You probably won't. **Often heard line:** "Let's dialogue."

The Insulter: She criticizes your intelligence, your appearance, your personal habits, your job, your family, etc. She may do this in public, for a laugh, and may think her jokes are just innocent fun. **Pros:** A little honest criticism can be an enlightening experience. **Cons:** Too much can be a demoralizing experience. **Often heard line:** "You're not exactly fat, but..."

The Internet Crazy: She e-mails you 24 hours a day. If you don't respond immediately, she freaks out and floods your inbox. When she gets angry, rather than confronting you, she sends you psycho e-mails written in all caps. **Pros:** If you're not into face-to-face confrontation, she's the woman for you. **Cons:** ARE YOU KIDDING??!!!! **Often heard line:** Nothing. She doesn't talk to you. She only sends e-mails.

The Jealous Lesbian: She needs to know where you are at all times. If you're having coffee with another woman, she drives by to make sure you didn't go to a motel with her instead. **Pros:** She will make you feel needed. **Cons:** She will make you feel herded. **Often heard line:** "Whose number is this on your cell phone?"

The Kowtower: When you get into an argument, she always backs down. When you ask her where she wants to go for dinner, she says, "Wherever you want to go." **Pros:** She will do whatever you ask her to do. **Cons:** You'll lose respect for her—and fast. Then one day, she'll snap. **Often heard line:** "I agree."

The Know-It-All: You tell her you went to Paris, she belts out a 20-minute discourse on the court of Louis XIV. You bring up something in the news, she corrects you left and right. She blabs and blabs and blabs, impressing you with her knowledge and massive lung capacity. If she pays for dinner, she lets her MENSA membership card fall out onto the table as she pulls her credit card from her Harvard insignia wallet. **Pros:** You may learn a lot. **Cons:** That's what libraries are for. **Often heard line:** Whatever it is, it's probably with an affected accent.

The Large-Group Awareness-Training Addict: She attends life-changing "meetings" and spends the majority of her time volunteering as a workshop facilitator or recruiting mentally ill people with trust funds off skid row. She'll constantly try to recruit you, and if you refuse to join, she'll gape at you in bewilderment and pity. When you say the word "cult," she gets defensive—even if you're talking about something entirely unrelated, like Charles Manson's impending parole date. **Pros:** She may be enlightened, to some degree—in a weird sort of way. **Cons:** You'll be disturbed by her frequently glazed expression. **Often heard line:** "There's this weeklong retreat..."

The Late Bloomer: Ah, the late bloomer. She may be in her 40s and married to a man, but she has recently made a "discovery" about her true sexual orientation. In fact, you may have been the one to bring her out. **Pros:** Knowing you brought someone out is a good feeling. **Cons:** She may go through a candy-store phase, where she can't be faithful to you because you're the first woman she's ever been with and she needs "to know what's out there." **Often heard line:** "Let's go to the [lesbian event] tonight!"

The Lesbian Without a Past: You ask her about her childhood, she changes the topic. You ask her where she went to college, she asks you to pass the salt. Basically, you have no clue who she is because she's hiding something—perhaps something big like a criminal record or history of conning people. **Pros:** Makes an excellent listener, and how often do you find someone who's always turning the conversation back to you? **Cons:** You'll never be able to trust her. **Often heard line:** "I can't discuss that (accompanied by a long pregnant pause)."

The Love Addict: She's in love with being in love. Thirty seconds into your first date, she tells you she loves you. Before your second date (which you never even made with her), she showers you with gifts. **Pros:** For those who've never been told "I love you" before, she'll definitely fit the bill.**Cons:** Once the magic wears off, she'll be looking for someone else to cast her spell on. **Often heard line:** "I know I barely know you, but I feel like we're soul mates."

The Magical Thinker: Magical thinkers think like this: *If I pass a blue house in the next five minutes, Cathy will fall in love with me.* Or, *If it rains today, Mariah will call and ask me to get back together with her.* **Pros:** She's a girl who believes in destiny. **Cons:** Visiting hours at the sanitarium can be rather restrictive. **Occasionally heard line:** "Find a penny, pick it up...must hold my bank teller at gunpoint today."

The Master Manipulator: She's a master at getting you to do things for her. May use blackmail, guilt trips, even hypnotic techniques to get her way. **Pros:** Great in bed. **Cons:** Often too busy manipulating people to be interested in going to bed. **Often heard line:** "You don't really love me."

The Mindfucker: "I was hanging with this woman," said Amy, "who was financially very comfortable. Once she asked me to accompany her to all of these pricey grocers so she could buy ingredients to make this really nice dinner. As we shopped she went on and on about the recipe she was using. When we were done, she said, 'Well, that was fun. I've got to start cooking now. I'll call you in a couple of days.' She was making dinner for herself?!" The mindfucker is what her name implies. **Pros:** Perfect for emotional masochists and sexual submissives. **Cons:** Your brain may implode. **Often heard line:** "You don't mind, do you?"

The Mindreader: She tries to read the mind of every girl she dates. She'll phone her friends and say, "Barb didn't call today. What do you think that means?" Before you can answer, she'll go into an hour-long analysis of the situation, all based on conjecture. **Pros:** If you're not much of a conversationalist, your pal will fill in the silences. **Cons:** Her opinions are a gigantic waste of time. **Often heard line:** "Tracy's going to break up with me. I just know it."

The Mistruster: She keeps tabs on you because she thinks you're sleeping around. She needs to know where you are at all times. She may covertly follow you. She may check your credit card statements and cell phone bill. No matter how many times you assure her of your fidelity, she won't believe you. **Pros:** At least you know she cares. **Cons:** Caring can have an evil side. **Often heard line:** "I know where you were last night."

The Misunderstood Artist: Oh, woe is her. She writes gloomy poetry. She goes to cafés to brood and smoke clove cigarettes. She constantly complains that no one truly understands her. She's got a major victim attitude and may spend long hours in her garage-turned-studio listening to Tori Amos CDs. **Pros:** You may go down with her in the annals of artistic history. **Cons:** These types are rarely talented. **Often heard line:** "I'm in a Frida Kahlo phase."

The Mobster: She hangs around construction sites with guys named Vinnie and Big Lou. **Pros:** Lots of big Italian dinners. **Cons:** If you piss her off, you'll be swimming with da fishes. **Often heard line:** "I gotta go down to da loading dock."

The Narcissist: She spends three hours getting ready for work. Every time she passes a mirror, she checks her lipstick. She's always asking you for your opinion because she craves your approval and compliments. She probably never asks you about you; when you do talk about yourself, she quickly changes the subject. **Pros:** It's nice to have a well put-together, attractive babe on your arm. **Cons:** She's as insecure as a shanty in a typhoon. **Often heard line:** "Am I fuckable, or what?"

The "No Boundaries" Freak: This woman may encapsulate many other types, including the Love Addict, the Internet Crazy, the Manipulator, the Googler, and the Drunk. She has no sense of where she ends and others begin. She may stalk you, get drunk, and make out with women in public places, or spread lies about you. **Pros:** If you have no boundaries, you'll become one gigantic blobby blur with this woman. And, if you have no boundaries, this sounds pretty damn appealing to you. **Cons:** Your every waking moment will be a big disgusting mess. **Often heard line:** "I read your journal."

The Note Writer: Note writers are afraid of confrontation, but what they aren't afraid of is writing 20-page dissertations on why you should recycle or why the dog needs a bath, even when a simple verbal request would suffice. But for Note Writers, no verbal request is simple or easy, so they spill their guts on paper. **Pros:** The written word can be quite lovely. **Cons:** Annoying and unnecessarily time consuming with someone you see at least eight out of every 16 waking hours per day. **Often read line:** "I feel I have to tell you..."

The Nymphomaniac: She wants to have sex 24/7. **Pros:** Mama mia! **Cons:** When she gets bored with you or when you won't put out, she'll look elsewhere. **Often heard line:** "I'm a slave to my libido."

The Obsessive Caller: Get yourself caller ID, girlfriend, because you'll need it with this one. **Pros:** You'll constantly be in touch. **Cons:** You'll constantly be in touch. **Often heard line:** "Did you get my fax?"

The Obsessed Married Woman: She may be straight, bisexual, closeted, or just curious, but whatever she is, she's obsessed with you. Even if you're not interested, she won't let up...and she won't leave her husband either. **Pros:** If you're Jeannette Winterson, sleeping with a married woman can be a huge turn-on. **Cons:** What goes around comes around. **Often heard line:** "Bill's on a business trip again..."

The Ogler: When you're out on the town, she stares at other women and is often completely oblivious about her behavior. **Pros:** If you're into three-ways, maybe she can catch a cute girl's eye. **Cons:** It's completely (1) embarrassing; (2) demoralizing; (3) belittling; (4) upsetting. **Often heard line:** "What? Are you kidding me? I was looking at her boots."

Ol' Dead Eyes: You'll probably never hook up with this type because she'll scare the bejesus out of you on your first date. The only way to explain it is that when you look at her, you see nothing in her eyes. Nada. The windows to the soul are closed. **Pros:** If prolonged eye contact makes you nervous, or if you're a chronic ogler, Ol' Dead Eyes may fit the bill. **Cons:** Zombies eat brains! **Often heard line:** "Brains..."

The One-Date Stalker: You tell her you don't want to go on a second date and she sends you angry e-mails written in all caps, camps out on your lawn, and begs you to go out with her again. She may also send you strange gifts to get you to fall in love with her—such as a recycled gas-bill envelope containing a sprig of rosemary and three of her baby teeth. **Pros:** Who doesn't love a fan? **Cons:** When Kathy Bates said "I'm your number 1 fan" in the film *Misery,* James Caan ended up with two broken ankles. **Often heard line:** "Give me a chance."

The Perpetual Dater: She goes on a few dates with a woman then moves on to the next one. She's looking for someone who's perfect, and none of the women she dates meet all of her criteria. **Pros:** If you just want to have sex, she might give up one or two of her criteria and go for it. **Cons:** If by some strange fluke she does end up in a relationship with you, it'll end when she finds out something minor about you that wasn't at first obvious—such as the fact that you're a twin or allergic to peanut oil. **Often heard line:** "My friends say I'm too picky, but damn it, I deserve the best!"

The Perpetual PMSer: She can't go hiking with you because she has cramps. She's too bloated to go dancing. Her tits are sore. Blah, blah, blah. She complains of these symptoms 23 days out of the month. **Pros:** You'll spend lots of time applying hot water bottles to her lower abdomen in bed. **Cons:** You'll never have sex in that bed again because you'll associate it with a hospital ward. **Often heard line:** "Don't touch me there."

The Public Massager: This one is just plain gross. When you go to a party, she can be found in the corner of the room massaging her friend Donna's stiff shoulders. At work she sidles up to coworkers to relieve their back pain. If she's a physical or massage therapist, she may make bogus excuses about her behavior to you ("I'm trying to keep my skills honed," etc.). **Pros:** If you can get her to massage you all the time, who cares? **Cons:** It's so creepy seeing people massaged in public, especially when it's your girlfriend doing it to someone else. **Often heard line:** "Where's the sesame body oil?" (said at Shakey's Pizza Restaurant).

The Rescuer: She's thrilled when you lose your job, need a $500 loan, or your car battery dies, because that means she can swoop in like SuperDyke and save your ass. She gets such a high off rescuing you and in the worst case scenario she may even create disastrous circumstances so she can do just that. **Pros:** Often these types are good-hearted and actually will help you when you need it the most. **Cons:** Often these types are codependent and hold long-term grudges or use their good deeds against you at a later date. **Often heard line:** "You don't appreciate a single thing I do for you."

The Sad Sack: She's Eeyore and Debbie Downer rolled into one. **Pros:** When you're around her, you'll feel grateful you're a fairly content person. **Cons:** More than likely, she'll drag you down, and you'll spend most of your time trying to cheer her up. **Often heard line:** "I'm sad and tired. And tired of being sad and tired." (**Note:** She may be clinically depressed, which is no joking matter. If you suspect this, suggest she consult a psychiatrist or other mental health professional.)

The Serial Monogamist: Her biological "move on" clock is scheduled to go off any second now. **Pros:** If you're also a serial monogamist, you two will be happy together—for five minutes. **Cons:** You'll end up watching her settle down with every girl in town—for five minutes. **Often heard line:** "I feel like a horse that was never meant to be bridled."

The Sick Partner: The sick partner is never well. She always has something wrong with her, be it a prolonged case of the runs, plantar fasciitis, myofascial pain, toenail fungus, migraines, cramps, depression, or all of the above. **Pros:** She'll make you feel needed. **Cons:** Her ailments may be used as an excuse not to do things, keeping the two of you stuck at home in a codependent nightmare. **Often heard line:** "Can you pick up my drops on the way home? And can you cancel our dinner with the Finches?"

The Serious Lesbian: Somewhere along the road to forming her philosophical and political convictions, this lesbian lost her sense of humor. Having memorized the basic tenets of feminism, separatism, vegetarianism, and 12-step recovery, she has dedicated her life to following and enforcing them. Sometimes she does this as an activist or academic, but mainly she does this *one lesbian at a time.* **Pros:** Finally someone who'll take you seriously. **Cons**: She stamps out fun like nobody's business. **Often heard line:** "Chicken *is* meat."

The Slacker: She wants you to pay for everything because she refuses to get a job. If she has a job, it's a part-time telemarketing gig and she calls in sick half the time. She's constantly late with the rent money and rarely if ever apologizes. **Pros:** If you get off on being in control, you're in the right relationship. **Cons:** Who wants to be taken advantage of? **Often heard line:** "I'll have the money on Wednesday."

The Sloth: She may claim she has chronic fatigue syndrome or Epstein-Barr, even though she's never been diagnosed or visited a doctor. Her favorite thing to do is watch TV Land all weekend. **Pros:** If you're a caretaker type, she's for you. **Cons:** Who wants to waste her life watching *Sanford and Son* reruns? **Often heard line:** "I'm taking a nap."

The Tale-Teller: If there's a problem in your relationship, she talks to mutual friends about it instead of talking with you. **Pros:** At least you won't have to listen to all her bullshit. **Cons:** You'll find yourself wondering, *Why don't our friends invite us to do anything anymore?* **Often heard line:** "I'm going over to Sheila's."

The Tarot Reader: Wondering how to heal your relationship? Wondering if you two have a future together? She's got the answer: It's in the cards. **Pros:** If you leave it all up to the cards, you don't have to take any responsibility for the outcome. **Cons:** This crap gets old fast. **Often heard line:** "The Hanged Man, Queen of Pentacles, and Page of Cups in the Three Fates spread means we'll make that tofu dish you like tonight."

The Therapy Addict: Can't even hiccup without asking her therapist what it means. **Pros:** Maybe you'll get some insight into why you got involved with this woman in the first place. **Cons:** Stepford-wife parroting can be grating and mind-numbing. **Often heard line:** "I see *my* therapist daily, so I don't see why you can't too."

The Thrower: This kind of behavior may be mild, such as her tossing something small when she gets upset, or she may throw larger objects (a radio, the television, your dog) at the wall in a crazy fit. **Pros:** Makes a great center fielder. **Cons:** Her behavior may escalate from mild throwing to full-on throwing. Try to help her curb it so it doesn't spiral out of control. You don't want to end up with a concussion—or worse. **Often heard line:** "Where's the Super Glue?"

The U-Haul Dyke: She moved in with her last girlfriend after a month. And the one before that. And the one before that. Her live-in stints usually last five to six months before she looks for someone new to fill the huge hole in her life. **Pros:** It's always good to know a girl who drives a truck... **Cons:** You may have to load the truck. **Often heard line:** "Where'd you put the dolly?"

The Unitopical: No, this does not mean she has one eyebrow. It means she's obsessed with one topic only and spends the majority of her time discussing it—be it her mother, her nightmare boss, the ozone layer, or the roles of gender, race, and class in Victorian culture. **Pros:** In a short time, you'll be a master in one subject. **Cons:** Being with this woman is like living inside a music box playing "Three Blind Mice" 24/7. Sooner or later you're going to lose it—and when you do, it'll be U-G-L-Y. **Often heard line:** "Are you even *listening* to me?"

The Workaholic Multitasker: "Sorry, can't make it Tuesday. I've got a dental appointment *and* a conference call. Nope, Wednesday's not good either—I'm taking some clients to a Laker game. Thursday? No can do." **Pros:** If you need a lot of space in a relationship, you've met the right woman. **Cons:** Do you really want a relationship with someone you only see once a month? **Often heard line:** "Let me check my BlackBerry."

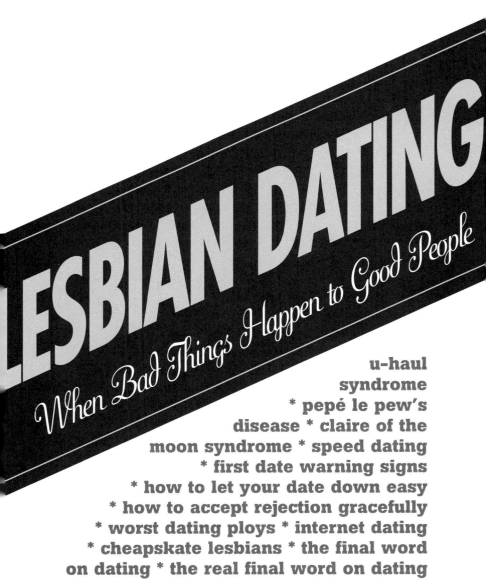

LESBIAN DATING

When Bad Things Happen to Good People

u-haul
syndrome
* pepé le pew's
disease * claire of the
moon syndrome * speed dating
* first date warning signs
* how to let your date down easy
* how to accept rejection gracefully
* worst dating ploys * internet dating
* cheapskate lesbians * the final word
on dating * the real final word on dating

"She took me to an event at a womyn-only, chem-free, smoke-free, man-free, shirt-free, S/M-free space. I'll tell you one thing...it sure wasn't a 'bongos-free' space." —Anne

"We had arranged to meet at a coffee house. When I got there, I asked her if she wanted anything to drink. She pointed to a boozy-smelling green plastic travel mug on the table and said, 'No, I brought my own slushy drink I made at home.'" —Angela B.

Dating is like a Ferris wheel: It's thrilling when you first get on, yet as those sweeping circles continue, you're either amazed at the beauty and splendor of the experience or puking blue cotton candy over the guardrail and wondering if it'll ever end. Although dating is hard for everybody, a few distinctive tendencies give dyke dating a special brand of chaos. To prevent serious drama, you've got to know what you're dealing with.

Of course, just putting the word *dating* in this chapter title significantly ignores the fact that many dykes never even get the word *date*. "In the old days," says Lisa E. Davis, seasoned dyke-drama survivor and author of the historical mystery novel *Under the Mink,* "there was no such thing as lesbian dating. You just went to the bar and bought a girl a drink, then if all went well, you slept with her. There was no dating, and I don't see why we should start doing it now. Back then it was much simpler."

This chapter will help you maneuver around the pitfalls of dyke dating—from avoiding total nutjobs to letting gals down easy to handling rejection. If, after reading this chapter, you still think dating is thrilling—and you aren't ready to hurl over the guardrail—more power to you.

Diseases of the Heart

Before we get into the nitty-gritty, it's first necessary to review the various illnesses, diseases, and syndromes that plague courting lesbians. Whether you're a deep-in-the-trenches pro or a dyke-dating novice, the following section will help you spot some subtle—and not-so-subtle—red flags from a mile away.

U-Haul Syndrome (UHS)

The urge to move in together on the second date is an oft-touted norm of lesbian life. But our unchecked nesting instincts can get us into serious trouble. Julie B. in Portland met her first girlfriend in a bar and went home with her two dates later. They spent the weekend making "passionate love." Then, finding they were unable to pry themselves apart, they moved in together. Only when it was too late did Julie learn about her new lover's drug problem. Not only was Julie already emotionally involved, but the two were seriously financially entangled. "I skipped the dating phase and signed up for a yearlong nightmare that included a serious car crash, having to fight off my crazed crack-fiend girlfriend for the last $40 in my wallet, going hungry, wandering the streets homeless, and other bullshit!" (And that's just *Julie's* side of the story!)

The term "U-Haul Syndrome" is a nod to the abject poverty of many lesbians. (Otherwise it'd be called "Swank Moving Company Syndrome.") This term goes hand-in-hand with the stereotype (see "Corky" in the movie *Bound*) that all of us can fix our own cars. Duh, it's not because we don't want to depend on men (who can't fix cars either), it's because we don't have the green to hire an actual mechanic. Anyway, our financial woes are often a precipitating factor in moving in together too early, which makes it even harder to separate when things go bad. I remember having such a mean case of sciatica that the mere thought of having to fork over another 50 bucks I didn't have, plus reload and unload another U-Haul, made me clutch my aching back muscles, grit my teeth, and stick it out for another six months with an ex of mine who will forever be referred to as "the baby talker from hell."

Keep in mind that the U-Haul is only partly a reference to poverty. The main part is still about moving in too hastily. Having the bucks to spring for the luxury of a squad of movers doesn't preclude you from suffering the fall-out of a poor choice

of partners. The more money you have, the more likely you are to be milked, bilked, or slapped with an ugly galimony suit. Once we win the right to marry, she can rake you over the coals in real live divorce court.

Not all U-Haul trips end in disaster, though. Amid a slew of shakily scrawled horror stories, I received a shocking bit of testimony from one of my many dyke-drama survey takers: "I met my ex in July, we moved in together in August, and we were together for four years. It was the best and longest relationship I ever had." Before the knee-jerk reaction to suggest that the operative word here is *had,* and that *rose-colored glasses* are clearly this woman's favorite fashion accessory, it's necessary to understand how and why this freak occurrence occurred. Given that for the longest time in our history this was our preferred method of hooking up (not counting the convent, concubine household, prison, or all-girl boarding school, because in these situations—hello!—cohabitation came even *before* the first date), you're bound to have a few successes. Some dykes do beat the odds.

Pepé Le Pew's Disease (PLPD)

Remember Pepé Le Pew, the crazy cartoon skunk who just didn't know when to back off? No matter how hard that little black feline tried to squirm free or claw Pepé's eyes out, Pepé was convinced it was all just a ploy, the lady-skunk version of playing hard to get. We lesbians do this on a subtler scale—by hanging back in the wings and pining for someone who never intends to go out with us. In severe cases of PLPD, the love-struck dyke interprets all signs of rejection as containing hidden signs of true love. She puts her whole life on hold, refusing to date other women while she waits for her object of desire to come around.

She may wind up a stalker (see chapter titled "Dyke Stalkers"). Or she may just carry around a faded picture of the woman for the rest of her lonely life and not say a word to her. Ever.

Claire of the Moon Syndrome (CMS)
(Formerly *Desert Hearts* Disease)

This antithesis to the U-Haul Syndrome is often seen when one or both parties are in the closet, or when lesbians decide to make a movie. Courtships that last more than two to three months will frustrate everyone involved, including observers or audiences. Two women are attracted to each other but just can't admit it. Instead they have "chance" encounters charged with animosity and laden with embarrassingly tacky innuendo. They drink a lot whenever together, each hoping to be held unaccountable when the other one finally makes a move—or else, a movie. Unfortunately, neither is up to the task.

Unfinished Business Illness (UBI)

Sheila drives her date, Renni, back to Renni's apartment after a simply marvelous evening, and once she pulls up to the curb the two begin to kiss. Seven minutes later, with blouses agape and hair askew, the two manage to pull back and stare deeply into each other's eyes. Renni, who once habitually chewed her hair in grammar school, now brushes a few strands out of her mouth that had fallen in when she lowered her eyes to give Sheila "the look." The look was plagiarized from Prince circa *Purple Rain,* and—in Renni's version—involves sucking in her cheeks while emanating a funky and wild sensuality that increases when she concentrates on the word *funktastic*.

"Wish you could come up," Renni says meaningfully, and Sheila replies, "Is that your way of asking me to come up?"

"Well...if that means you're interested in coming up..."

"That depends on whether you really are inviting me ..."

"So if I were inviting you, you'd say...?"

"Yes," Sheila says. "I'd say yes, I am really interested in coming up."

(Sheila is about to discover Renni has UBI!)

"There's one small problem," says Renni. "My ex is still living with me, and we have an agreement about bringing people into what was once our home...so," she brightens, "we *could* go to your place..."

Sheila's house is a mess. She hasn't emptied the litter box in weeks. "How about we just sneak into your place quietly? It's late enough."

"Well, actually, we only have a one-bedroom apartment, so I don't have my own room. I'm sleeping on the couch (a white lie—she's still sleeping in the same bed with her ex) for now."

When the ex still figures prominently in your new girl's life, she's got UBI, and you've got a solid case of Class III dyke drama on your hands. RUN!

Organized Group Activity Dating Disorder (OGADD, pronounced "Oh, Gawd!")

Fear of leaving the safety of the coven features heavily in this disorder, which occurs when a lesbian or entire circle of lesbians becomes psychologically addicted to the communal environment and refuses to date one-on-one. She will go on planned group dates only, such as organized moonlit hikes, women's folk music karaoke nights, and women's basketball outings. Most group-dating junkies have two characteristics in common: They were part of a support group during their coming-out process and have been on at least one Olivia cruise.

Speed Dating

Lesbian speed dating has always seemed like a bad idea to me. Don't lesbians need to slow things down? Speed dating sounds like what I've done all my life. Do I really need someone to facilitate it for me? What I'd really like to see facilitated is something called "slow dating." Instead of making lesbians switch partners every seven minutes, put two women face-to-face for one week in a slab of concrete with a couple of drainage holes, then break them out and see if they still want to switch partners. Gourmet meals provided.

So You're Finally Out on a Real Date, Now What?

Listing qualities you value in a person and being aware of them while on a date is a fine idea, but without proper antennae for the things that can go wrong, you may as well just bite yourself in the ass right now. The warning signs below won't necessarily rule out continuing to date such a person, but at least you can go in with your eyes wide open.

First Date Warning Signs and What They Signify

1. She applies Neosporin to her lips, openly complaining of "dryness," or pulls other total gross-out maneuvers. *Diagnosis:* Fear of intimacy leads her to subconsciously repulse her date.

2. She maintains uncomfortably prolonged eye contact. *Diagnosis:* no boundaries.

3. She brings more than one gift. *Diagnosis:* compensating for something.

4. She's a poor listener and a perseverative speaker. *Diagnosis:* narcissistic personality disorder.

5. She dangles material possessions as if to lure you in. *Diagnosis:* low self-esteem.

6. She has more than two pets. *Diagnosis:* animal addiction.

7. She's a graduate student. *Diagnosis:* won't have time for you.

8. She lies about being a smoker. *Diagnosis:* a smoking liar!

9. She's in an "open" relationship or dating more than one person. *Diagnosis:* commitmentphobe (often most attractive to monogamous women).

10. She isn't out of the closet yet. *Diagnosis:* due for a nervous breakdown.

11. She tells multiple stories about friends who've wronged her, then moves on to her family, her employer, the government, and finally the system. *Diagnosis:* victim mentality (will soon be telling the same stories about you).

12. She spends a lot of time talking about her ex, or has been breaking up with the same woman for the last seven years. *Diagnosis:* Unfinished Business Illness.

13. She stands up in the middle of dinner to perform a series of yoga poses. *Diagnosis:* She's *wack.*

Of course, a lesbian may decide she doesn't care about finding a relationship and simply wants to get laid. However, once she sleeps with another woman she may find herself in a state of premature in-the-sack elation, a condition that renders her giddy—which is a good thing—but, sadly, incapable of making sound judgments, which can lead to the sudden onset of U-Haul Syndrome.

Leslie Lange

Emergency Intervention:
How to Prevent Premature In-the-Sack Elation:

Take a time-out break to call your mother. Ask her if *she* thinks it's wise to go home with the sexy P.E. teacher you've only just met. She probably won't think so, and this is even more likely when Mom doesn't yet know you're gay. Regardless, the sound of a mother's voice will likely diffuse any sexual tension.

World's Worst Lesbian Pick-Up Maneuvers

"The girlfriend of my girlfriend's best friend asked me if I'd give her a ride on my motorcycle. As I drove her around town, she held tightly to my waist, her hands occasionally straying toward my breasts, and shouted over the noise of the engine that we should get together once we had each broken up with our respective partners." —Teresa M.

Dyke Drama

"A frosted-mullet-wearing execu-dyke slips my girl her card and says, 'When you're ready to move up from the loading dock to the front office, call me.' " —J.D.

"One woman tried to be my friend when I was breaking up with someone—just so she could get me into bed." —Mia D.

"A classmate invited me for dinner and answered the door in a long satin bathrobe." —Bethany R.

"I used to work the door at a gay bar in the South with a biweekly drag show. The other woman who worked the door with me was older than my mother and had a thing for me and was always trying to ask me out by telling me about the mammoth dildos she owned. One night she was telling somebody in line that I was a virgin and she was going to break me in and then said to me, 'Isn't that right, Heather?' My name is not Heather so it was fairly ridiculous and not exactly suave." —Bridget C.

Leslie Lange

How to Let Your Date Down Easy

Let's say you've avoided sleeping with a smoker prematurely and decided that, since you have serious asthma, a smoker isn't quite the right gal for your future. Failing to return her phone calls is rude. Brutal honesty may get you blacklisted in the lesbian community, especially if the woman is well liked. How do you know how to go about it right?

• **DO NOT use e-mail.** Nothing said in an e-mail can ever fail to be insulting. This is the universal law of e-mail, and it is never to be scoffed at.

• **DO use white lies,** such as "I've realized suddenly I'm not quite ready to start dating again after all."

• **DO NOT use stupid white lies.** You can always tell a lie by its abundance of detail. Stupid lies are long lies. For example: "I've realized suddenly I'm not quite ready to start dating again after all. Another six years of celibacy, in a stone hut, in Ireland, should do it." Stupid white lies are driven by guilt. Get a grip.

• **DO sit with the guilt.** Don't act to alleviate it. Feeling guilty for rejecting someone you don't even like is a **reverse indicator.** A reverse indicator is a negative feeling that arises when you do something right, but your bad upbringing has conditioned you to think it's wrong. In the case of a lot of women, who are conditioned to protect other people's feelings ahead of their own, guilt is a common reverse indicator.

72

How to Accept Rejection Gracefully

- **ACCEPT that she will and should lie to spare your feelings,** and don't get mad if you catch her in one. If she tells you she's already seen *Shrek 2,* but then you spot her a week later in the audience with a small child, don't freak out. The sting in your ego will soon dissipate.

- **DO NOT try to "stay friends."** This can only lead to a friendship in which one person has all the power, a prolonged dynamic in which one ego gets fed and you keep pining and hoping.

- **RESIST the urge to keep trying.** Suck it up. And for Pete's sake, show some pride.

- **DO NOT interpret silence for fear,** wanting to take it slow, etc... Interested people will make it clear. If you're not sure, *be blunt and ask.*

- **DO NOT stalk her.** Resist the urge to drive by her house or hang out for hours at her favorite café.

- If she goes out on a date with you, then tells you she's realized she's not really ready for a relationship, **DO NOT check her Internet personal ad** to see if she's still looking for someone.

- **OBEY the rule of two refusals:** If she turns down two invitations, it's up to her to renew the invitation.

- **REPEAT** one of the following sour-grapes mantras: "It's a good thing it didn't work out—smart, funny, and beautiful women are so high-maintenance." "There's someone better around the corner, I just know it!" And "She's probably bad in bed." **DO NOT** share these mantras with others. They're for private use only.

Leslie Lange

WORST DATING PLOYS

I'M DYING.

(HAS A SERIOUS ADDICTION OR ANOREXIA NERVOSA.)

I THINK I MAY HAVE AN UNTREATED MENTAL ILLNESS.

(SHE JUST WON'T TAKE HER MEDS.)

I LOVE YOU, BUT I LOVE A LOT OF PEOPLE.

(--AND THE NEXT ONE WILL BE HERE ANY MINUTE, SO PLEASE LEAVE.)

MY EX IS STALKING ME!

(OWES HER EX A LARGE SUM OF MONEY.)

Dating and the Closet

Those who date while in the closet lead a schizophrenic existence. J.B. in Chicago went on a first date with a girl who wasn't out. They bumped into a group of the woman's close friends at a restaurant and they all had dinner together. "No one had any idea who I was," said J.B., "or why I was even there."

Suddenly J.B. also had no idea who she was or why she was there either.

Bringing Her Out

Despite the mythology of the lesbian predator, I have never met a dyke who truly relishes the idea of bringing someone out. By someone, I mean a *straight girl*. "It's just too damn risky, you know," griped my scuba instructor, Sally, as we chatted during a break at the edge of the pool. "She either completely shuns you afterward, or falls head over heels in love with you but then hates you for making her gay." Despite her distaste for the subject, Sally has brought out more women than any lesbian I know. In fact, I've never heard her talk about dating a lesbian who actually *has* any experience. I asked Sally if she could give me a rundown of the pitfalls of bringing someone out. She complied with a charming but haggard smile.

Initiation Pitfalls
(What May Happen When You Bring a Gal Out)
• She falls hard. Be prepared for this. If you don't fall in love with her, she can and will stalk you.
• She has "You're the Only One Syndrome": "I'm not gay. I just love *you*!"
• She blames you for making her gay. If you accept this cockamamy head trip, she may guilt you into doing things for her, like staying with her forever, or covering up the murder of her landlord.
• Her family blames you for making her gay.
• Her family is part of the Armenian mafia and blames you for making her gay. (This one really happened!)
• She takes turns sleeping with you and her ex-boyfriend or husband as a form of comparison shopping.
• She's really straight. The sex is bad. She uses you to make her boyfriend jealous, or worse, to titillate him and add spice to their boring sex life. You start to feel like a human sex toy. She arranges for her boyfriend to show up and watch.

Sally had a lot to say on the subject of bringing someone out. (I stopped telling lesbians I was writing a book on dyke drama a long time ago because it so often snaps their little mouths shut. Instead I ask questions as if I'm interested—you know, as a friend—and then secretly click on my new digital micro recorder from Radio Shack.) Her tips integrated nicely with some other sources, such as lesbian self-help books, my own experiences, and those really gross books for men on how to score with chicks.

**How to Bring Someone Out
(Safety Tips From a Certified Scuba Instructor)**
- Play hard to get. Do not pursue. Make her do all the work. A woman who has never had an experience with another woman will often engage in the most audacious flirting, all while still convinced of her heterosexuality. Your job is to wait until she completely humbles herself and is practically a nervous wreck. This rule is especially important when you are falling in love with her.
- Be prepared to show her the time of her life. Have plenty of lube on hand—and a spare set of batteries.
- Be prepared to stay up all night, or as well the case may be, to stay in all day—and the next night and the next day as well. You may have trouble getting her to let you leave (or getting her to leave). In these cases, you may have to make a deal with her or promise to return in ten minutes. Ten minutes later call her on your cell phone and tell her something came up...like your life.
- She may murmur the words "I love you" during her first sexual experience with you. This is a common brain lapse. Do not take it literally.
- Do not expect her to be good.
- Do not be surprised if she's a Pillow Princess at first.
- Do not be surprised if she's a natural, or even better in bed than you are. Count your blessings. Do not accuse her of lying about her experience with women.
- If she belongs to a conservative religious sect, or has gangsta

connections, take pains to prevent the possibility of violent retaliation by her people.

- Do not panic. Maintain a healthy tolerance of and detachment from the emotional upheavals she may experience during her coming-out process.
- Don't be a dyke-drama queen. Let the little things go.
- Be willing to get hurt. There are no surefire rules to protect yourself. This is not a Disneyland ride. This is life.

------------------------------✍-------------------------------

True Testimonial:
One Lesbian's Story of Dating a Closeted Woman

"She attended a lesbian discussion group, which is where we met. She wouldn't tell anybody where she worked and would only talk about her occupation in the vaguest, most meaningless way. She made good money, had a luxury apartment, and drove a high-priced Mercedes, but there was this secret agent-type atmosphere about it, and it wasn't attractive. It felt to me like more of a withholding, controlling kind of thing, driven by fear and, I think, self-importance. It was very annoying, going out to dinner (which we only did in a foreign country, Canada—so as not to run into anybody who knew her) or for a drive, knowing she was always on her guard not to say stuff about where she worked, or where her parents lived. As if I (or any other date) would someday walk into the office or her ancestral home and out her or something." —Lillian

------------------------------❦-------------------------------

Internet Dating

The Internet seems like a great way to meet your soul mate. You write down your likes and dislikes, she writes down hers, one of you spots the other's profile, and *presto!* instant love. Being enamored with this idea, Ronni S. developed what she believed to be a foolproof Internet dating system: First, she'd exchange e-mails with the other woman for a while, then go out with her for coffee, followed by whatever dates might come out of it. "Yeah, dream on!" said Ronni. "I never got farther than the first coffee. No second dates. Zero. Nil. The reason? They lied." One woman told Ronni she was "totally out," only to reveal in their first coffee date that she described herself as a "heterosexual looking for sex with a woman." One was old enough to be Ronni's mother, even though Ronni had specified she was looking for women in their 50s, like her. One said she was "athletic in appearance."

"Yeah, as far as a barn door can be athletic," Ronni lamented.

If the women weren't lying, there were other problems. One wouldn't stop talking, for example (which obviously would never show up in an e-mail). And three were "very sweet," but there was absolutely no chemistry.

Remember, the eyes—not a computer screen—are the window to the soul. When you're hungry to find love, it's easy to project your fantasies on to some gal you've never met. Internet daters often lie about their looks because they want to feel good about how they look. Don't act so scandalized! This is no different than trying to put one's best qualities forward during a date. A woman with a violent temper isn't likely to reveal this on a first date either. Ultimately, what's on the inside can be much scarier than what's on the outside anyway.

10 Internet Ad Warning Signs

- Her photo looks like it's from a high school yearbook (potted plants in the background, seated on wicker furniture, class of '74 printed in the corner).
- There *is* no photo.

- The ad states "not opposed to moving for the right person" (meaning she has no steady job or roots, and a U-Haul rental place is nearby, so...).
- She has no pets. There's something emotionally wrong with a lesbian who doesn't like animals. Period.
- She has too many pets. (Love for animals is one thing. Living waist-high in poop and having your vet bills send you to the poor house is another.)
- She mentions the word *recovering.*
- She includes the phrase *I've been burned/hurt, before...* .
- She describes her "ideal" first date. (Who can live up to "you: giggling and slapping my ass; me: picking out a pumpkin and kissing you under the stars on a hayride"?)
- She includes poetry. Good or bad, any poetry in an ad must be avoided.
- The fact that the ad is on the Internet is a deterrent in and of itself.

If you're determined to date via the Internet, keep expectations low. Internet dating is a very inefficient way to find a compatible partner. Expect several misses for every "hit." Be honest in your profile. The truth will come out eventually. Do not Photoshop your image or use a photo that does not accurately reflect the way you look now. It's the equivalent of a balding man's comb-over. Do not assume that a steamy instant-message exchange will equal sexual chemistry in a face-to-face encounter.

"I once met this foreign poet online," says Tina H. "We really hit it off on e-mail and phone and had long and sometimes erotic conversations. But when we met there was a total lack of chemistry. We could barely talk to each other. I had made it clear that I liked feminine women, and she looked like Beethoven."

Always be kind to those who disappoint you. If you spot your date before she spots you and she's not what you expected, never ever just disappear. Those who act with emotional maturity are those who truly deserve love.

Internet dating is not for everyone. Meeting other lesbians through people you know, or while doing what you enjoy, is still the best way to go.

True Testimonial:
One Lesbian's Internet Date Is Too Tacky to Be Believed!

"A woman I met online named Gail and I agreed to meet at a restaurant in downtown Denver one night for dinner. After spending considerable time primping I waited in the lobby for a while. Finally, a nice-looking woman with a little girl in tow approached me. She said Gail couldn't make it, that she had to go to a party, and that she had sent her, Stacy, instead to meet with me. Stacy was also a lesbian, and the little girl was Stacy's daughter. I thought this was some weird setup and declined to have dinner with the woman and her daughter.

Later, Gail called me and asked how dinner was. I was a bit upset and said, 'You stood me up to go to a party? How tacky.' It turned out that it wasn't just any party. It was her ex's new girlfriend's election victory party, because the ex's new girlfriend had just been elected state senator or some such thing. Apparently, Gail and her ex and her ex's lover all share a house (she assured me that it was a 'really big house'), and Gail and her ex own a mortgage business together. Gail had been instrumental in getting her ex's new lover elected, and her ex's new lover threw a fit when she heard that Gail had a prior engagement and wouldn't be coming to the party.

I asked Gail if she and her ex got along, since they still worked together and lived together. She said, 'I hate her.'"

I eventually agreed to meet Gail at a coffee shop (I have an unusual name and didn't want to get smeared in the local lesbian community as some flake—now I'm not sure why I was so worried). She was very strange. She told me she had a crush on her UPS driver, and mainly she wanted to meet me because I was 41 (at the time) and so was the UPS driver. Huh? Then she said she'd like to meet a woman who wanted to have a baby, but that she wanted her partner to be the surrogate mother, carrying an embryo made up of Gail's egg and some guy's sperm. I SWEAR THIS IS A TRUE STORY.

And remember her ex, the one she lives with and hates? She concluded the coffee date by asking me if I'd like to go to a cooking class that she, her ex, and her ex's new flame had signed up for. Oh, my God, I still get e-mails from her asking if I want to refinance through her mortgage company." —Melissande

True Testimonial:
One Lesbian's Internet Date
Turns Into a Surreal Nightmare

"There isn't much drama in Internet dating," said Jennifer K, a boom operator in the film industry, "That is, until you meet in person." Jennifer posted an ad on the Internet, hooked up with a gal, and agreed to meet her one afternoon...

"After lunch, we walked through Ferndell, a park named for its small ponds and many ferns. Dorit was very buoyant and had energy to spare. She told me she was a past-life regression therapist. I had fun with her because she was so off the wall. After walking through the park, she suggested we go to a Thai supermarket in Hollywood. Dorit ran around the market showing me all the unusual items and bargains to be had. During our little hike in Ferndell, she told me she was holding out for a blond goddess. I couldn't help her with this. We met again to go see some stand-up comedy. We talked on the phone and e-mailed. I started to feel comfortable seeing her. I met her brother and several of her friends. I would not let her regress me. From what she told me it involved hypnotism and she was certified.

Leslie Lange

I invited her to my home. She brought a precooked chicken. I had some salad and vegetables and we improvised a quick meal. I took her to see the beautiful 60-foot trees that surround the wood deck behind my house. She started to run to every tree, giving each a hug and invoking some kind of special communion with each tree. This really pissed me off because the back deck is my sacred space where I write and draw and sit for hours listening. I told her to leave the trees alone.

She mentioned something about wanting to pee right then and there. I told her to go in the house and use the bathroom. She was pulling at her pants. 'You're not peeing in my yard,' I implored her. We went inside and made dinner. I pointed out the bathroom and said, 'Go ahead.'

While I was making a salad, she snuck outside. I saw her come in the front door. 'You didn't?!' I said.

'Just a little,' she smiled.

I couldn't believe she had just peed in my yard! I'm just glad I didn't see it. What animal was she in a past life? She sensed I was upset. I showed her some recent books I'd purchased online. I let her borrow my book on Reiki healing. I walked her out to her car and gave a little wave. The words 'crazy bitch' went through my head.

Don't bother returning the book was my last thought as I turned away. I blamed myself for not having the foresight. Her eyes shone a little too brightly when she talked about herself. She had aspirations of changing the world. She was a real know-it-all. She told me I ate the wrong foods and listened to music that made me depressed. Her business card read: SPIRITUAL COACH. Although I'd like my Reiki book back, I never called her again."

Cheapskate Lesbians

I hope this doesn't offend anyone, but immediately after a nice dinner in a fancy (i.e., expensive) restaurant, I often feel a strong urge to go to the restroom. When I get back to the table, someone invariably accuses me of trying to "duck the bill," which I guess—at least subconsciously—is true. (It isn't me who's cheap, though, it's my intestines.) Oh, well. At least I'm not alone in this behavior: According to an important dyke-drama survey (mine), there are tons of cheapskate lesbians out there. "Get enough dykes together at a restaurant," says lesbian novelist Therese Szymanski, "all on one tab, and you're gonna end up short. Someone's gonna gyp the bill—but if you pay attention enough, you'll soon figure out who she is."

Sisters, I pray I never dine with lesbian novelist Therese Szymanski. She'd bust me faster than a speeding mullet.

Cheapskate behavior can be an indication of emotional stinginess. If she haggles over the bill, she may also save up her partner's minor offenses and mistakes, compiling a list in her head that enables her to feel justified in her own bad behaviors. Being a cheapskate is no fun. Being an emotional cheapskate is even worse. Dating a cheapskate? Proceed with caution.

DON'T DATE NO CHEAP, CHEAP DYKES

"A woman asked me to go to Solvang for the weekend then didn't have enough money for the hotel, so I paid because I was already there. Then she said, "So, are you buying me dinner?" I did the first night because she drove, but the next day I told her I'd buy my dinner and she could either buy her own or wash dishes." —Mia D.

"She wouldn't pay a quarter for the Magic Fingers mattress in the hotel room." —Paula N.

Leslie Lange

"Anytime we went to the supermarket, she'd pull all the groceries aside after checkout and compare the receipt to her purchases, item by item." —Ellen O.

"I cannot, repeat, CANNOT stand when I'm on a date with someone and they pick apart the check at a restaurant down to the cent. It's nuts. It also drives me crazy when they only want to give a 10% tip. I say just split the damn bill, even if your date ordered something more expensive." —Angela B.

"I once had a girl charge me for my half of dinner and a cab and later learned she'd expensed them to her office." —Trixi

"She refused to buy me an ice cream cone." —Bett W.

The Final Word on Dating

Dating is like a cup of coffee—it's ruined if it isn't the way you like it, like if there's too much cream or not enough or a floating speck you can't identify but that turns out to have eight hairy legs with suction cups at the end. If you don't like the first sip, you're a fool to drink the rest. However, don't blame the coffee. The coffee is right for someone, just not you. Don't be so fussy about your coffee that you stop enjoying it altogether. Newsflash: There is no "perfect" cup.

Because dating is so much like coffee, I recommend doing something besides "coffee" on your first date. Many lesbians have trouble telling the difference between "coffee" and "dating." But I'm not going to dwell on this subject because there's an entire book written about it already: *Is It a Date or Just Coffee? The Gay Girl's Guide to Dating, Sex, and Romance,* by Mo Brownsey. It's not as good as this book, but it's worth a look.

The Real Final Word on Dating

OK, the truth: I don't know a damn thing about dating or coffee. No one does. We all just do the best we can.

Dyke STALKERS

what is
stalking?
* sympathy for the
devil * the histrionic
victim * the stalker keeper *
dueling restraining orders * straight
woman stalking * nipping it in the bud *
totemic behavior * i'm no stalker, i'm just
in love! * you're probably a dangerous
lesbian stalker when... *
seven steps to stalker recovery

"I have been stalked by practically every woman I've had a relationship with." —Mia D.

Stalking's bad, OK? No one should ever stalk. Stalking is giving in to a delusion. Delusional thinking is related to depression: The fantasy keeps you sustained—and safe from your unhappiness. Stalking is a waste of time. You could be getting some nice therapy instead. Stalking is bad for your self-esteem.

What Is Stalking?

Stalking crosses all levels of class, race, and social standing. At its root, stalking involves initiating and maintaining unwanted contact. This includes making annoying phone calls (yes, your friendly telemarketer *is* stalking you); sending notes, e-mails, and instant messages (yes, your mother is also stalking you); giving gifts; shadowing, spying, or enlisting surveillance professionals (you *know* John Ashcroft is stalking you); and conducting obsessive Internet research, also known as Googling. Romantic stalking is the same stuff done in the name of love, and it can provoke various gut reactions in the victim, including fear, anger, or even a hysterical thrill (like "Ooh, cooties!" mixed with "Ooh, but at least somebody thinks I'm attractive!" or "I can't wait to tell my friends!").

Many types of stalkers exist, from the everyday pest to the scary-ass psycho-killer. Some are rejected ex-lovers, seesawing back and forth between attempts to reconcile and attempts to exact cold-blooded revenge. Some are deluded into thinking the stalked woman is—or at least once was—in love with them, even in cases of minimal contact. Some are just clods who've seen too many Hollywood movies and have no manners and are too lazy or too stupid to understand subtle communications such as "Please go away now." And a rare few take pleasure in the torture of the hunt. In the beginning, there's no way to tell one from the other—and that should really give you the goose bumps.

Sympathy for the Devil

Despite a propensity to judge political, culinary, and sexual practices, lesbians often let their guards down in the face of an obsessive female stalker. We get all hung up on how tough being a woman is—and we know how easy it is to get your head all screwed up over some hot lady librarian or sure-handed fire-fighter. What lesbian hasn't traveled a twisted path? Who am I to judge the closeted woman with no other outlet for her romantic feelings? Or the woman whose childhood abuse (or myriad other factors) has left her with a poor sense of self-esteem and no boundaries? And moreover, why fault the woman with wisdom enough to dedicate her full attention to worshipping me? Lesbian (or at least bi) stalkers make for great scary movies (see *The Hunger, Single White Female,* and *Basic Instinct*). They also make for great "B" stories on sitcoms and television dramas (see Tammy Lynn Michaels on *The L Word*). And while lesbians do stalk, and do kill—they are much less likely to do so than heterosexual males. Why worry?

This empathy for our stalkers (*She reminds me of my mom!*) mixed with the pleasure of being adored (*She's giving me what Mom never gave!*) may inhibit some women from setting limits early. And early limits are just what's needed. For the good of all, the stalker's behavior should be nipped in the bud.

The bad news is, the female stalker is harder to detect than her male counterpart. Your average dyke may never know she's being stalked, or may not find out until it's far too late and she's got her hands (and e-mail account) full. Women, after all, make very good spies. We're used to being what others expect—lesbians even more so. We've watched Barbara Feldon's every move on *Get Smart,* and we keep things close to the vest—especially those of us fond of wearing vests. The good news is, if you never know you're being stalked, you will never know you're being stalked, and if you never know you're being stalked, you'll never be bothered by it. If there is such a thing as an ethical stalker, it would be the undetected stalker, the stalker who does not disrupt the life of the person she's stalking.

The Histrionic Victim

No dyke worth her dramatic salt keeps her stalker a secret. She regales her friends with multiple phone calls, multiple pleas for advice, and multiple renditions of her stalker's latest activities:

"She sent me a card with a teddy bear on the front! Can you believe it? I'm kind of wondering if I should dig up that old pistol, you know, and apply for a carrier's permit?"

"She's lurking around in the parking lot again...wait a minute, I need to go look out the window real quick."

"She was in the cafeteria today, making googly eyes at me from across the room."

"She said hello."

Sometimes all this attention gets to be too much for a girl. She gets sucked into the maelstrom and leaves her brain far behind. Once I let my friend Melinda crash at my apartment for a week. She said she needed a break from her stalker. Late one night the phone rang, and I heard Melinda having a somewhat angry conversation. Thirty minutes later a woman wearing white overalls and a purple beret was standing on the lawn outside my window calling out, "Melinda, Melinda..." A few minutes later I heard the front door open, and the next thing I knew there was a screaming match going on in my kitchen. That's when I realized what I know now: My friend was in love with the drama of being stalked. She was a "stalker keeper."

How to Help a Friend (or Lover) Who's a Stalker Keeper

- Do not reward her with extra attention or sympathy when she talks about her stalker.
- Write down the number of a local victim's assistance center on several scraps of paper and hand her one every time she ,brings it up.
- Refer her to the Stalking Resource Center Web site at www.ncvc.org/src. (No, this is not a how-to site!)

Dueling Restraining Orders

Sometimes exes get so mad they take out multiple restraining orders against each other while living in the same house! When this happens it's sometimes necessary for the legal system and all local victims' assistance programs (a.k.a. threat management teams) to take out their own restraining orders against each ex. If this is unsuccessful, the only solution is to place them in separate but equal booby hatches.

Stalked by Your Ex's New Lover?

Unbeknownst to you, your latest ex has been talking you up to her new lover, a woman who was recently released from prison after serving a term for armed robbery. One day the phone rings:

"Hi, this is Jerri." (so-and-so's new lover!)

"Hi, Jerri."

"So-and-so left me."

"Oh. I'm sorry."

"She said she'd leave me if I started drinking again. And I don't know where she i-i-is. Is she with you?"

"No."

"Are you sure?"

"Yes."

"Well, do you know how to get hold of her?"

"Not if she's disappeared."

"Well," says Jerri. "If she contacts you...um...'cause she's not there, right? Anyway, if she contacts you, could you give her a message from me?"

Sigh. "Sure."

"OK, can you tell her I need to tell her something?"

"OK. Sure."

Twenty minutes later, the phone rings again. "Hi, it's Jerri. Did she contact you yet?"

When the new love of an old ex contacts you, you are under no obligation to help or discuss any of her problems.

Terminate the phone call immediately and do not answer any letters or e-mails.

Straight Woman Stalking

Sometimes the dyke stalker isn't a dyke at all—not yet at least. The closeted still-calling-herself-straight woman is perhaps the wackiest of same-sex stalkers. Her desire has been flying so far under the radar for so long not even *she's* aware of it anymore. She often compensates by being overly—and overtly!—hetero-feminine, a heavily made-up, pink pantsuit-wearing parody, what Gloria Steinem has dubbed the "female drag queen."

Emergency Intervention:
When Your Stalker Has a Gun

Your stalker drives up, rolls down her window, aims an assault rifle in your direction, and shouts, "Get in!" You should:

(a) Run! Run toward the rear of the car—it's hardest to fire a gun in that direction—then continue running in a zigzag pattern.
(b) Get in the car and pretend to be in love with her so as to buy time to formulate an escape plan.
(c) Ask her to marry you, because anyone who cares that much is worth keeping.
(d) Attempt to disarm her: A swift kick or slap to the muzzle will knock the gun from her hands.
Answer: (a)

Leslie Lange

Whatever you call her—however she dresses, does her face, or walks—she's a straight-looking, straight-acting, bona fide wish-I-were-a-lesbian ticking time bomb! One day, somehow, somewhere, some lesbian is going to be a little bit kind to her, or just sort of polite, and *boom!* she's in love.

And not just any old ordinary kind of love, but a really scary, psychotic kind of love. Is she in love with this particular lesbian, or what this lesbian represents: the self she could be if only she gave herself permission to accept her love of poontang?

Terrifyingly unpredictable, the repressed lesbian is capable of any number of immature passes. Having buried her sexual desire since childhood, she has the romantic maturity of a seven-year-old. We all know why lesbian desire may become repressed: A woman lives in a hostile environment, such as an impoverished hyperreligious community, or perhaps she holds a high-profile, high-responsibility position in a male-dominated field (police officer, corporate CEO, etc.). Maybe her father is a senator or, hell, the president even. The closet is a factory for lesbian stalkers. So is helplessness, depression, and delusion.

Lorelie W., a speech therapist for a major metropolitan school district, remembers being stalked by Viola, the department office assistant. (Years later, the assistant blamed her behavior on a taboo imposed by her inner city community's strict Baptist teachings.) "Strangely enough, it all started with *me* being intrigued by *her*," Lorelie told me. "She draped herself in lime-green cotton-blend outfits, had long red-lacquered fingernails, and wore her hair in a tight bun. Whenever anyone entered the room, Viola would just freeze and only her eyes would move. She reminded me of a giant gecko trying to camouflage itself. She was clearly depressed, but there was something fascinating to me about it, like, how could she be so depressed and do so little around the office and still keep her job?" Lorelie tried to perk up "the depressive straight woman." She made little jokes and teased her until she started to come round. She complimented Viola on her lime-green clothes. Then one day Lorelie entered the office and Viola's stern bun had changed. "She'd had extensions put in, and it was like where the bun used to be there was now this spiraling fountain of hair flowing out, with a streak of bright purple running through it." The two women had another conversation. "She told me about her recent divorce, her abusive husband, and these tickets they had won to Jamaica," Lorelie said. "She needed to find someone to go with her. 'I want to take someone real special...' she said. I thought to myself, *Does she mean me?*"

Not long after, Lorelie—who was in a relationship at the time—received her first of several anonymous letters:

DEAR LOVELY LORELIE,
COME TO THE ISLAND WITH ME AND WE WILL MAKE BEAUTI-
FUL LOVE ALL NIGHT LONG.
WITH LOVE,
YOUR SECRET ADMIRER

P.S. BRING IMODIUM AD JUST IN CASE. YOU KNOW HOW THE
WATER IS IN THOSE PLACES.

When Lorelie got more unwanted mail she fortunately knew what to do. She took the letters to her supervisor in a sealed Rubbermaid container (to preserve any fingerprints), then went directly to Viola and asked her if she knew who was sending the letters. Viola denied doing it, but Lorelie told her she really wished they would stop. They did. Now ten years later, Viola lives in South Florida with her new lesbian lover, a cop she met on the Internet.

Leslie Lange

Nipping It in the Bud

Stalking is always more complicated than it seems. The cliché of the pathetic but violent white male with an "if I can't have you nobody can" chip on his shoulder has become a stale metaphor for the consequences of living in a male-dominated society. Stalking in the news almost always consists of a murder-suicide, compliments of the ex boyfriend or husband, with a history of multiple restraining orders and a bit of wailing over the futility of our system and its failure to protect women. But what can we do when women are the very people we need to be protected from?

------------------------------✍----------------------------

True Testimonial:
One Lesbian Who Dealt With
Her Stalker the Right Way

"A very sweet little old woman about 20 years my senior decided she was in love with me although we'd barely had any contact at all. She also decided that I needed protection from who-knows-what, so she made herself my guardian. She began 'patrolling' my house, calling at unusual hours, and sending me gifts. I asked her to stop the contacts, and I returned her gifts and reminded her of the stalking laws in our state. She sent one last, very expensive gift to me with a letter that read: 'I know you will return this. There is only one way. You must bring it to my house [she included directions]. If you don't you will make me do something we will both feel very sorry about. Sweet. I contacted the police who assured her that there was indeed another way to return the gift and said she must never have contact with me again. I never heard from her again." —Ronni S.

----------------------------❧----------------------------

Steps to Prevent Stalking:

1. Trust your gut, even if it sometimes grumbles inappropriately.

2. Be aware: Do not overlook any unwanted attention.

3. Nip things in the bud with direct and firm communication: no mixed messages. This does not mean you need to insult her. This does mean you can't "be friends."

4. Be disciplined about discontinuing contact with this woman. If you get angry or give in, it's like reinforcing the bad behavior of a lab rat. If you take advantage of her crush on you to get her to help you move your refrigerator or write a term paper for you, expect the worst. Maintain zero contact.

5. If you've asked her not to call you and she does, repeatedly, do not under any circumstances call her back. Do not ask her for favors or do favors for her. This includes your psycho ex.

6. Document, document, document. Save letters. Burn a CD of her phone messages (if you can figure out how to do this, you're a genius!), and hang on to them for a while.

If You're Already Being Stalked:

1. Follow the above steps, but consult an experienced "threat management team." More information is available through the Stalking Resource Center Web site (www.ncvc.org/src).

2. Do not flirt as a way to appease your stalker. Do not appease your stalker period.

Leslie Lange

3. Confront your stalker as soon as possible, one time only. Do not insult her.

4. Take your stalker seriously. Do not use her antics as entertainment for your friends, nor as a way to inflate your popularity or perceived desirability to others.

5. Do not underestimate the potential for escalation in her behavior (trained professionals may assist with this). By the same token, try to resist paranoia (I personally have found that a couple of Xanax and a Bud Light may assist with this).

6. If you go to a safe house, don't leave her a slip of paper with your new address on it—especially if your safe house is the home of a friend (see section on the "Histrionic Victim" in this chapter).

7. You may need to file a restraining order. This should be done only after consulting a professional threat management team who may help you determine if filing a restraining order is overkill, or if it is only going to piss her off more.

8. If you *do* file a restraining order, this *does not* mean you should prance around in front of your stalker chanting, "I got a restraining order...I got a restraining order...." I hope I don't need to explain why.

The Attorney General for each of the 50 states should offer info on local programs. Local law enforcement, mental health centers, and justice centers can also provide referrals. If you're concerned these centers may not take your concerns seriously because you're a lesbian, contact the Stalking Resource Center at src@ncvc.org or (202) 467-8700.

"A restraining order should be pursued only after seeking assistance from an objective party (threat management team). A restraining order may actually escalate stalking events or provide victims with a false sense of security and lead to carelessness." —Stalking Resource Center Web site

---

Totemic Behavior

Totemic behavior is a lesser form of stalking, driven by the emotional masochism of the woman who practices it. A totem is, of course, usually an animal or plant that serves as the emblem of a certain family or affiliation, such as the turquoise bear worn by Aunt Mildred in Santa Fe, which expresses her belonging to a tribe of affluent blue-haired retirees who go around calling people "honey" a lot. In the case of the totemic lesbian stalker, the totem is usually the home of her ex-lover at around 10 or 11 P.M. on Friday, which expresses her belonging to a tribe of tortured rejects.

Totemic stalking is an addiction to the emotional pain of rejection. Driving over to the object's home produces a flurry of anxiety. *What if her car's not there? Is*

she on a date? What if her car is there, but there's someone in there with her? What if there's no one there with her but she's still happier without me? What if she sees me drive by? Then she'll really know I'm a loser. Nothing hammers home one's lack of success, one's complete lack of a life, than giving in to a drive-by.

Totemic stalkers have telltale faces: The mouth is frowny. The eyes are puffy. The cheeks sometimes shine under a thin brine of tear salt.

What to Do If You're a "Drive-By Ex-Lover"

Some women will be able to stop themselves through sheer force of will once the sadness has worn off and the need to feel it passes. A good friend may offer some tough-love advice such as: "Stop driving by this woman's house! Go home, cry alone, and get over it." And this is sometimes enough.

Like many items of mystical significance, the home of one's intended soul mate may exercise a hold on your psyche that is impossible to break without professional help. The assistance of a licensed totem-worker (there are several listings in the Taos, New Mexico, Yellow Pages) may be a costly but wise investment. If you don't have the funds, or just don't go in for all that goofy spirituality stuff, there's one other surefire way to stop drive-bys: Get caught. Nothing will make you feel more ridiculous than this.

I Want a Piece of You Near Me

One step beyond the drive-by is the abduction of an object owned by your beloved. This may be something she touched only briefly, such as the discarded Starbucks napkin used to wipe cappuccino foam from her lips, or something she's owned for many years, such as a pair of eyebrow tweezers...or her ear.

Hester P. claimed to have pilfered a lipstick-smudged pillowcase from a floor-sample bed at Macy's where the stalkee was shopping with her current partner.

Alaska lesbian Mary W. had a rather unsettling experience when someone climbed through her window and took her reading glasses from the nightstand. "Her name was Babs!" exclaimed Mary. "And she was the premier real estate agent in the area. For years I wondered, *Why the glasses?* But I never found out."

I'm No Stalker—I'm Just in Love!

With all the many forms of stalking, it's sometimes hard to tell if you're doing something really bad or if you're just in love. When "I can't stop thinking about Lulu" becomes "I can't stop sending psychic messages to Lulu," you may still be in the "no harm, no foul" zone. When it becomes "I must kidnap Lulu and tie her up in a cabin," that's crossing a line.

You're Probably a Dangerous Lesbian Stalker When...

- As a top mail-order client, you receive a free $50 gift certificate good toward camouflage wear, night-vision goggles, and listening devices from Cabela's hunting supply catalog. They throw in a free box of valerian-root powder—great for spiking herbal tea.
- Your phone bill is exceptionally low because all your outgoing calls are hangups.
- You call Gump's stationery department to ask if they carry "anonymous note cards" in lavender
- Your computer tracks all of her e-mails, travel plans, and banking activity because you're terrified she'll flee the continent to get rid of you.
- You've been showing up at the same Starbucks every day for a month, all because you heard *she* went there once—six years ago.

Leslie Lange

- Someone's going way out of her way to avoid you, and you're not just imagining it.
- You send imaginative gifts—a rainbow-colored rose bouquet, a See's candy sampler, a severed head—and she *still* won't go out with you. What's her problem?
- There is no such thing as too much ammo.
- The latest restraining order gets tossed (unopened) into the slush pile.
- You quit your job to devote your full attention to the object of your desire. Every morning you take a bus to your car and sit in it—outside her apartment.
- Your DVD collection is laden with such titles as *Single White Female, Fatal Attraction, The Hunger,* and *Misery.* You see the female stalkers as compelling protagonists and the uncooperative objects of their affection as unsympathetic antagonists.
- You composed a folk song praising John Hinckley Jr. as an honorary lesbian.
- You pray daily at a homemade shrine made with pieces of her hair and other stolen fetish items. You burn "love spell" candles and look for signs in the sky.

Seven Steps to Stalker Recovery

1. Think of yourself as a quality person.
2. Talk to a therapist who can help you to do this.
3. Find a hobby—stalking not being it. Fun activities you might enjoy include constructing a dollhouse (where you can keep a colorful cast of characters who stalk each other) and playing *The Sims* video game.
4. Confront your stalkee to make your feelings known. If she rejects you, move on. Do not second-guess her. This is known as "the healthy way of dealing with things."

Dyke Drama

5. If you think she's the only woman you could ever love, head for your local gay and lesbian center.

6. Move to another state.

7. Talk to friends about the problem. The less secretive you are about your behavior, the more likely you are to be grounded in reality—the exception being the enabling friend who comes up with all kinds of creative ideas about how she can help you stalk your object of desire.

Obsessive love is normal, but giving in to the urge to stalk is childish—and will take you to the dark side.

Reading List

The Gift of Fear and Other Survival Signals That Protect Us From Violence, by Gavin De Becker (Dell, 1998)

I Know You Really Love Me: A Psychiatrist's Journal of Erotomania, Stalking, and Obsessive Love, by Doreen R. Orion (Macmillan General Reference, 1997)

The Psychology of Stalking: Clinical and Forensic Perspectives, edited by J. Reid Meloy (Academic Press, 1998)

Safety for Stalking Victims: How to Save Your Privacy, Your Sanity, and Your Life, by Lyn Bates (Writer's Showcase Press, 2001)

Surviving a Stalker: Everything You Need to Know to Keep Yourself Safe, by Linden Gross (Marlowe and Company, 2000)

Violent Attachments, by J. Reid Meloy (Rowman and Littlefield Publishers, 1997)

Advanced Reading List

Holiday Stalking Stuffers, by Phillipa Pakage (Pursuit Press, 2003)

Pipi Longstalking, by Atta Distance (Binocular Books, 2004)

Leslie Lange

Relationship

DRAMA

the
dark side
revealed * double
pms * 10 ways to
thwart a girlfriend's urge to
move in with you too soon
* single white female syndrome *
codependence * lesbian bed death * the
land of over-processing * lesbian predators
* the drama couple * newcomer phenomenon* couples counseling * family planning
* tips for healthy lesbian relationships

"I hate relationship drama. I hate affairs that hurt people's feelings. I hate getting involved with people's friends. I hate cliques of any kind. I tend to get involved with people that none of my friends know. The down side is that they often end up being Russian mail-order brides I meet on Hollywood Boulevard."
—Bett W.

Some of us never get lucky enough to land in a relationship. For those of us who do, it's a common delusion to believe all our woman-centered woes have ended. But we're simply in for a new brand of dyke drama—more domesticated, yes, but no less confusing. The shift is in trying to maintain the illusion as more and more flaws move from hinter into the foreground. Passion fades. You get by on memories of passion. Then one night you stare out the corner of one eye in disbelief at her complacent figure draped in the raggedy beige flannel pajamas her mother rescued from last year's Memorial Day garage sale: This is the beginning of what is called "the relationship."

The Dark Side Revealed

So now you're a happy couple.

Sure, you won't have to worry about dates flaking on you, lying to you, or becoming obsessed with you, but you may discover something even scarier—that you yourself are a flake, a liar, a person who doesn't respect her partner's boundaries, and that you have a host of other ill-bred qualities she's all too willing to tell you about. These revelations go down even harder when you yourself start to see and point out (none too delicately) all of *her* flaws.

In the best of circumstances you'll discover mostly trivial

annoyances. She doesn't floss ("It hurts, and besides my mouth is too small...just ask my dentist, they have to use the child-size X-ray tabs..."). She has bad table manners ("I was raised by wolves..."). She's directionally impaired ("You're so tense it makes me so nervous, so I forget where I'm going..."). If you're not so lucky, she'll be hooked on smack, or she'll reveal that she fakes her orgasms (ouch), or that she expects you to fund her psychotherapy as well as the endangered insect docu-mentary she's been putting together for the last six years while not generating any income. You may learn that she uses a stolen handicapped parking placard. Or that she suddenly wants to give men a try...or Scientology. Whatever pushes your buttons most.

"I Sure Wish She'd Told Me This Before We Got Involved..."

"I once dated a bulimic who successfully hid this from me until I found the 800 ice cream containers in her car. She was also addicted to nasal spray, which she abused daily and frequently." —**Shelly**

"She was a home care nurse, and she would save up the morphine and other narcotics from her patients who'd died, and shoot up." —**Melissande**

"She swore she had been lovers with both Kate Jackson and Jodie Foster, told elaborate stories about her continuing relationships with them (Kate Jackson took care of her while she was having chemotherapy), and was so believable that people believed her for years." —anonymous

"She had excuses for everything, and if I called her on something—and I quoted her exact words to her—she'd say 'Stop twisting my words!' " —Mia D.

"She had a phobia of going down on me that she refused to work on." —Lorraine V.

Friend Neglect

The devastating discovery that your girlfriend is addicted to nasal spray can be made all the more disconcerting if by the time you realize it you have no friends left to complain to. The phenomenon of "friend neglect" occurs in all new relationships, but with our tendency to phagocytize each other (commonly known as "merging" or "codependence"), we dykes are at higher risk. We neglect to return phone calls, stop going to Sunday night *L Word* parties, and stay in bed feeding our new lover strawberries all weekend, missing out on fun-filled flag football games. We exist under the delusion that everything we need in life comes from one wonderful gal. And then, something just...happens. While brushing your teeth one morning you spy a six-inch pile of empty nasal spray canisters at the bottom of the bathroom wastebasket. You think: *Is this normal?* You need: a reality check.

You pick up the phone and dial the number of your best friend (what was her name again?). You receive a recorded message. Her number has been changed.

Staying in Touch With Friends

The most honest methods are often the most fruitful. At the beginning of a new lesbian romance, a form letter sent to all friends and exes is an excellent idea. Let your people know you care by anticipating their bitter disappointment and deflecting it with humor. Cheapskates who brave the expense of having the letter preprinted on fancy stationery from Gump's will win extra points. Instead of being mad at you, your pal will think, *Wow, this new lover must be something special indeed—wonder if she knows what she's getting into?*

Sample "I'm in Love" Announcement to Your Best Friends

```
Dear [best friend/ex/the one relative I'm
out to/etc.],
    I have fallen in love—yes, I know,
again—but it is every bit as intense as
last year's little fiasco, if not more.
Because of this malady, amphetamine-like
substances have flooded my brain. This is
a situation I have no control over; in fact,
it controls me. The good news is, this can
last a maximum of only four to seven months—
a single Yellowstone brown bear's hiberna-
tion phase—before a gradual dissipation, at
which point I will emerge disoriented and
contrite and really, really need you for a
reality check.
    During the interim, please forgive me
```

for not contacting you or for blowing you
off on your birthday or for any other
unfriend-like, unex-like, or unfamily-
like behavior. Most of all, please don't
see it as a reason to blow *me* off or forget *my* birthday, though I'd naturally
prefer all gifts to be sent by either mail
or personal courier. If you should have a
change of address or phone number during
this period, please do not hesitate to
forward it to me at my e-mail address (no
phone calls, please—not just yet!) at:
leslielange@leslielange.com.

With love,
(your smitten friend) Leslie

Double PMS

Pugs, scoops of ice cream...lots of things are nicer in twos—
but PMS isn't one of them. (In polite circles, the code for this is:
"Granted, we were both feeling a little under the weather that
day...") Much like dyke drama and lesbian bed death, the idio-
syncratically Sapphic Double PMS is something we'd rather not
acknowledge. If we do, aren't we contributing to the notion that
there's something intrinsically wrong with being a lesbian?
Don't we have enough to feel inadequate about? And where
does worrying get us? Why, it just makes us more neurotic. And
when that happens, who can tell where the actual syndrome
ends and the self-fulfilling prophecy begins? Whatever.

Everybody knows about those studies of women's dormito-
ries. When two or more females live and interact in proximity to
each other (see "merging"), they start menstruating around the
same time of the month, most often when the moon is full. Stiff

little hairs sprout on their upper lips and chins. They snarl and snap at each other like bloated she-wolves.

At my university, not only were the girls in my dorm wing menstruating together, they were getting it on in the showers too. Our alpha female was a giant, gorgeous Hawaiian softball dyke named Sugars. Sugars ran the show. Her hormones were like Pied Piper music to any young coed with a sprinkle of bi-dust in her hair. No matter how latent the tendency, one's vaginal walls felt tranquil in the presence of the Shugs. The hormones produced by her ovaries gave off a kind of supermusk that synchronized all uteruses within a seven-mile radius to her personal menstrual schedule. Even the local church ladies were onboard. My 72-year-old bank teller once mentioned to me a reversal of menopause that mystified her family doctor. Sugars was just that powerful.

Sugars was famous statewide for initiating the tradition of debuting all the lesbians on our university's softball team. This happened annually at a big party where everyone got drunk, then Sugars would proclaim her gayness and invite her teammates to do the same—to come forward without shame. Two by two, the couples came forth, holding hands, blushing. "I'm gay." "Me too." "So are we!" And so on, as the one straight woman on the team looked on in scandalized amusement.

Sugars was also known for her jealousy and violent temper, which had nothing to do with her menstrual cycle and everything to do with the stress of leading legions of collegiate athletes, PTA moms, and bank tellers into the lesbian fold. The pressures of being top uterus, you know.

But I digress.

The following examples illustrate how Double PMS can affect a couple's ability to resolve conflict in a healthy manner. In the first dialogue, neither woman has PMS. The second dialogue is one in which only one woman has it. The third reflects a classic lesbian version of Double PMS.

Dialogue 1 (PMS-Free):
Judy: How do I love you? Let me count the ways...
Gina: Is that from *Romeo and Juliet*?

Dialogue 2 (PMS Present in One Person):
Judy: How do I love you...?
Gina: Well, I thought you had enough of my advice!

Dialogue 3 (Double PMS):
Judy: You don't love me anymore!
Gina: Stop, stop, STOP!!! I can't take it anymore! (throws hands up, runs screaming from the room)

Ways to Enjoy Simultaneous PMS
- Enjoy a hot bath and a glass of red wine or some PMS tea together.
- Binge on dark chocolate.
- Have a dish-breaking party. Take turns shattering the good china in the kitchen sink.
- Haul out the big dildo.
- Take a day hike.
- Hire a massage therapist for a home visit to perform acupressure on your PMS points.
- Have a lip-and-chin-waxing party or enter a drag-king contest together.
- Call in sick, put on some baggy old sweatpants, and watch court shows all day.
- Keep a list of the top ten people you'd like to tell off. Sit down and take turns calling all of them together. Joint angry-letter-

writing sessions work wonders for many banshee-like symptoms and prevents the displacement of displaced anger on to one's partner.

• For bourgeois PMSers, buy matching Burberry hot water bottles.

Needy vs. Cranky

Not all of us get bitchy when we have PMS. Some of us get horny, and even more of us get needy. The needy PMSer is often in want of a foot massage, a Tylenol for her headache, or a nice cup of peppermint tea. She needs lots of extra sleep. She loves nothing better than to take a nap on the sofa with a hot water bottle on her tummy while you wait on her hand and foot. With double PMS, when there's one needy PMSer and one cranky PMSer, the cranky PMSer can satisfy her bitchy side by acting like a dominatrix nurse. Go ahead, wait on your needy girlfriend, but be gruff about it.

The needy-cranky complex is by far preferable to a double-needy situation, in which one woman will be just beginning to relax from her foot massage when she's suddenly asked to—gasp!—return the favor. This is when hiring a massage therapist to come over and do you both comes in handy. Another solution is to invest in a couple of mechanical massage chairs, the kind with heat-convection coils built in (which I've found come in handy as makeshift waffle warmers). Or one of you could get pregnant. Or one of you could leave town. Double-needy matchups should pick activities that soothe both women simultaneously. Don't be afraid of cliché. If sharing a hot bath, playing a Tracy Chapman album, and burning some lavender candles does the trick, go with it.

Music is very helpful in soothing the savage PMS beast. If you're crampy, get those magic (i.e., radioactive) heat packs that slip inside your panties. Eat well, take vitamins, and if all else fails, try antidepressants.

Living Together

Not all lesbian couples live together, but most do—and do it soon. Is it genetic? No one knows. What we do know is that, despite escalating housing costs, the emotional benefits of a warm body (bigger than a cat) to cuddle with each night, countless redundant CDs that can be sold for big bucks on eBay, and the feel-good-about-myself joy of rescuing a "poor waif with no place else to go," delaying cohabitation is one of the smartest choices a drama-prone dyke can make. Give yourself time to learn about this woman, for Pete's sake. You can't possibly know everything about her in less than a week. If she's pressuring you to move in—a warning sign in and of itself—there are a few surefire ways to slow her down.

10 Ways to Thwart a Girlfriend's Urge to Move in With You Too Soon (Of course, one should always try to reason with a person first, but if all reason fails, employ one or more of the following techniques.)

1.   Save up all your dirty laundry for a month, then place it in large piles around your apartment/house.

2.   Ask your friends to call you when she's over and pretend to be bill collectors, mental institution administrators, STD clinic workers, etc. Make sure the machine picks up and that the volume is on "high."

3.   Have your mother or other family members call and leave irate messages. Ask your ex (if you're on friendly terms) to do the same.

4. Redecorate your place with horrid artwork (Precious Moments figurines, Thomas Kinkade and Nagel prints, *Hustler* centerfolds, whatever will turn her off the most).

5. Convince her that U-Haul is a politically incorrect company, with investments in Third World countries guilty of severe human rights abuses.

6. If she's a vegetarian—whether garden-variety, lacto-ovo, pesco, or vegan—drastically change your diet to include one or more of the following items: Salisbury steak, pork chops, beef stroganoff, tripe, haggis, etc. Invite her over for dinner.

7. Adopt several large dogs with territory issues.

8. Tell her you've decided to turn your home into a halfway house, convent, orphanage, animal experimentation facility, New Age retreat, Log Cabin Republican headquarters, etc.

9. Tell her you're straight.

10. Move without saying a word.
(For information on the Federal Witness Protection Program visit www.usdoj.gov/marshals/factsheets/witsec02.htm.)

The Gift of Time

In the early stages of romance (called "limerance" by New Agey psychologists), the pituitary gland leaks a steady stream of amphetamine-like chemicals to your brain. It's good shit, all right, this lover's high, but such hormonal happiness is a major stunter of common sense. Suddenly, just about any bad habit is OK—no, more than OK, it's cute! I once thought it was "cute" that my lover drank her own urine for a year to balance her pH and strengthen her immune system, but do you think *that* lasted? Wait till this wears off—wait till you have that first little inkling of, "Hey, who turned off my morphine drip?"

Once you allow a healthy amount of time to pass before moving in together, you'll be glad you did. And what is a healthy amount of time? Time enough to allow the dark side to be revealed, time enough for you to weigh objectively whether her perpetual lateness, obsessive hand-washing, diet pill addiction, chronic unemployment, untreated clinical depression, and odd revelation that she sleeps with a rosary in one hand to ward off night attacks by vampires are quirks you think you can handle.

Single White Female Syndrome

The lesbian gene seems to give us the urge to merge, particularly in the area of wardrobe. We wear the same outfits, the same colors, the same shoes. This happens telepathically; we can be dressing in opposite rooms and the result is the same. It's demoralizing, constantly coming home from Old Navy with the same pair of cargo pants as your lover.

Another scary thing is when one or both partners start using the word *we* when referring only to herself. The drama starts when your friends begin to notice, or when one half of the couple becomes disturbed by this phenomenon while the other half does everything in her power to perpetuate it.

What about when your partner starts wearing *your* clothes all time? What about when she does it without asking? Does she dig your favorite sweater out of the clothes hamper with the lame excuse that it's only because it has your smell on it? Have you ruined more than one perfectly good bowling shirt in a tug of war? If so, it's time to start setting some limits.

Emergency Intervention:
Setting Wardrobe Limits

Place several slips of paper in a hat. On each slip of paper write down a different color. Take turns drawing colors with your partner until all the colors are allotted. Feel free to add stripes and paisley prints for fun. Do this exercise again, only with different types of fabrics on the slips of paper. This can be done with shoes (sandals, high tops, heels, etc.), personal styles (preppy, punk, hippie, cowgirl, etc.), and even hairdos.

Let's Be Codependent Together!

Codependence may start with a shared wardrobe, but its tendrils soon extend to every aspect of a lesbian couple's life. If you don't know what codependence means, you could try looking it up in the dictionary. If you're too much of a lazy ass to look it up, you could wait for me to tell you what it means, which would be very codependent of you, and which besides could prove a very long wait because I'm actually too much of a lazy ass myself to walk across the room right now and get the dictionary. Didn't codependence originally have something to do with being emotionally dependent on an addict? But then it evolved into something more like mutual dependence, but a really sick kind, right?

Right?

Leslie Lange

Hello, is anybody out there?

I know! Let's be codependent together and rely on the definitions I received from a bunch of lesbians I talked to!

Q: How would you define codependent?
A: Hold on, let me ask my girlfriend.

"You rent the U-haul and she drives it." —Paula N.

"I define codependent as someone who defines herself solely through her significant other; who can only discern her own value through having another person emotionally committed to her. That without a significant other, she feels that she herself is barely entitled to exist and/or be happy." —Marilyn L.

"You spend all your time with one person and never ever ever talk to or see anyone else—ever—oh, and you cry a lot." —Stacy R.

"I can take care of you far better than you can take care of you, and as long as I'm in control everything is good until, of course, it gets bad, which it will, because you want to take care of both you and me, and you just can't." —Ronni S.

"You know, this ain't such a bad thing if you're both mutually in love and codependent. But when you can't stand the woman, codependency feels like you got this leech on your back that just sucks the happiness out of life." —Adelina C.

"Codependency is when one partner cannot follow through on her life or plans without knowing what the other partner is doing. Every mood, idea, action is interconnected with those of her partner. It's something this culture trains women to be, and I think gets hyper-realized when two women are together because we relate so much more easily (socially and emotionally) than men and women do. It's like we think every lover is also our sister. And while she may be in the feminist context, we shouldn't be conjoined." —author Jewelle Gomez

"No boundaries. She acts as if my life is hers." —anonymous

"Two needs fitting like puzzle pieces, then exploding the whole puzzle." —Lexi K.

"She feeds off my insecurities and unhealthy needs, and I feed off her compulsion to take care of me." —Tabitha F.

"She won't let me walk down the street to buy cigarettes." —Bett W.

"Someone who could never just wait in the car at the grocery store." —Anne S.

"I have several friends, straight and queer, who have been diagnosed as codependent by the medical profession. As far as I can see, it means you can't wipe your own ass without asking someone else what they think of the action—if they approve of your wiping motion, what brand of toilet paper they prefer, why they look down on you for shitting in the first place, and why they keep judging your gastrointestinal tract." —Bridget C.

Lesbian Bed Death

Bed death is a widely known phenomenon, common not just for lesbians, but for all persons who expel gas, use the toilet, and floss in each other's presence. There are all sorts of ways to combat bed death: therapy; workshops; scheduled "sex dates"; and spicing things up with toys, role-play, and wearing prison garb or other politically incorrect costumes—but I'll leave this to the experts. As a nonexpert (drawing my conclusions from stereotype, invention, and hearsay) I believe a lot of the dyke drama experienced by those in relationships appears during the late phases of lesbian bed death. The condition should neither be ignored nor resignedly accepted. Do not try to wish it away. Seek help. Bed death sufferers are in a drama-prone state, vulnerable to outside seductions and marathons of psychobabble that reduce both partners to tearful mush heaps. Regrettable door-slamming theatrics are not uncommon.

How to Tell if You're in the Throes of Lesbian Bed Death
• Your bedroom door creaks...like the lid of a coffin.
• The flowers on your bedside table are wilted, but you have no urge to change them.
• You've forgotten what it tastes like—or what it even used to look like.
• Your sex toys have accumulated more dust than a useless piece of home gym equipment.
• You actually use that "massage tool" to massage your own feet.

The Five Phases of Lesbian Bed Death
1. **Denial:** "I'm going through the motions but *so* not into it."
2. **Bargaining:** "Maybe if we cut down on our sugar consumption and get more sleep, we'll be less fatigued and our chemistry will come back."

Dyke Drama

3. **Anger:** "Why? Why? Why?"

4. **Acceptance:** "OK, it's official. We are experiencing bed death and we both know it."

5. **Processing:** "The best way to deal with anything—per lesbian credo #687—is to talk about it. And talk about it, and talk about it, and talk about it... And the more you talk about it, the less you actually *do* it.

The So-Called "Lie" of Lesbian Bed Death

Many respected academics and professionals—social activists, psychologists, professors...serious lesbians, OK?—have attempted to debunk the so-called "myth of lesbian bed death," claiming the phenomenon is overblown and that even having a term like *lesbian bed death* attaches a stigma to being lesbian, leading to neurotic worrying, which I guess would make us too much like neurotic heterosexuals. No one would like to see the end of LBD more than I would. But solving it in my own relationship will not solve a damn thing for my community.

Rather than denying that lesbian bed death exists, we need to relieve ourselves of the stigma associated with it. Don't call it a death, call it the "lesbian sexual rejuvenation phase." Consider the beautiful imagery of the chrysalis...the caterpillar enters its cocoon to emerge as a butterfly. Consider the lull in your sex life as an opportunity to emerge as something even more beautiful—a beautiful lesbian butterfly, with each half of the couple represented by the wings. Done barfing yet? Good, let's move on.

The "lesbian sexual rejuvenation phase" is needed to recover from the "lesbian romance phase," which consists of trips to each other's homes or apartments with an overnight bag and pet carrier, sex till 2 or 3 A.M., and waking at 5 or 6 to return

Leslie Lange

Emergency Intervention:
Lesbian Bed Death

Desperate to reinfuse passion into your relationship? Start a raging quarrel with your partner. A large percentage of lesbian arguments lead to make-up sex, which has been reported by thousands of couples to be the hottest sex ever.

home to drop off the pet in time to be at work by 8. Feelings are so intense during this phase that a woman's life is totally put on hold. The "lesbian sexual rejuvenation phase" is just your life getting revenge on you for neglecting it for so long. Time to make up for all that lost sleep! Nothing more, nothing less than pure survival instinct.

So whenever you hear someone say she's experiencing lesbian bed death, or when you even so much as think those ugly words about your own relationship, substitute the term "lesbian sexual rejuvenation phase." It's as pleasant to say as "supercalifragilisticexpialidocious" and will ease your shame while lifting your spirits.

The Land of Over-Processing

If we weren't so damn neurotic about lesbian bed death we could welcome getting some extra sleep, taking a break from the seemingly endless frenzy of all-night sex marathons. But no, we miss the soaring high of it all, the self-affirmation only countless hours of stellar sex can deliver. Without all this we start to panic, and in our panic we do what all good lesbians are genetically programmed to do: We process.

Processing, ugh! We hate it, but we love it. Yes, we do. Texas policewomen, Becky and Michelle, once lay in bed for hours discussing in excruciating detail the deficiencies in Michelle's table manners. Wouldn't it have been better to discuss it that night at Roy's Barbeque, at the actual time Michelle was, in fact, talking with her mouth full (and in front of all their friends!)? Or immediately after dinner, in the privacy of Becky's car? Perhaps more time should have passed, and the subject would have been better broached the next morning as Becky served Michelle her morning coffee, waiting a few minutes for the caffeine to kick in. Or would it have been best to schedule an appointment to discuss such a hot-button issue? Note that in the above example the processing is essentially about when would be the best time to process. This is called "taking it to the next level."

Processing gets you everywhere and nowhere at the same time (which is pretty fucking profound, if you ask me). And if the art of processing is one of womankind's greatest achievements, then lesbian couples take it to the level of masterpiece: Not only do we process a subject to death, we do it until it's pureed beyond recognition. How can there *not* be a direct link between lesbian processing and lesbian bed death (now, of course, renamed the "lesbian sexual rejuvenation phase")? The connection is simple: Lesbians ultimately spend more time processing in bed than they do having sex in it.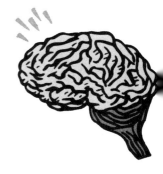

It's an established fact: Hours of sustained processing can cause temporary—and sometimes permanent—brain damage.

When a couple stays in bed processing through breakfast and lunch their heads become so empty of crucial nutrients that the discussion takes an insane tilt and morphs into a hysterical, sob-filled fight. Brain scans of lesbians in high processing mode show similarities to those of humans who've wandered lost in the woods for days in the late stages of hypothermia. In such cases, survival dictates that one half of the couple—whoever's strongest at this point—is sent out to forage. She scours the kitchen and ransacks her gym bag for anything of nutritive value—coffee, a stale energy bar, any sort of quick pick-me-up that can bring about a return to normal brain wave patterns.

When this sort of thing happens with increasing regularity, as it *always* does in lesbian relationships, it's inevitable that the favored place of processing—i.e., the bed—would come to represent starvation rather than a place to enjoy sex. Even couples with powerful physical chemistry begin to associate the bed and being in it with a helpless place of blurred boundaries where proper nourishment is withheld. A reverse Pavlovian response develops out of this association, so that when the couple does climb into bed together, they immediately want to fall asleep—not to consciously avoid sex but to avoid another bout of processing.

Lesbians can diminish the effects of this connection by (a) having more sex outside of the bed; (b) processing only in special predesignated areas; and (c) never skipping a meal.

Taking it to the Next Level With Processing—Academia-Style

"I was seeing a self-described lesbian-identified bisexual Jew. She allowed that she had never experienced any actual sexual desire or attraction toward men, but she felt bisexuals were discounted by the gay community at large, and that by identifying as bisexual she could understand what it felt like to be 'marginalized within the margins.' She was careful to point out that the modifier 'lesbian-identified' made it clear she was totally down with her lesbianism and that she wasn't identifying as bisexual in order to compromise her Kinsey-6 queer identity in any way. One night we were having sex in her twin bed—never an easy proposition—when her roommate entered the room unannounced. We bolted upright, and Hannah [not her real name] yelled at her roommate, now joined by her girlfriend, to get out of her bedroom. 'Not until you help us settle a dispute,' the roommate said. To my surprise and frustration, Hannah heard them out. It seems the girlfriend had called the roommate 'exotically beautiful,' and the roommate, who was from India, by way of Sacramento, wanted Hannah to tell the girlfriend, a fellow Jew, why what she said was offensive to her and all people of color, and why Jews, 'of all people,' should understand. Hannah entered the zone: We got dressed and went to the living room to discuss how the subliminal messages of patriarchal whiteness perpetuate the subaltern status of the 'other.' By the time the conversation flagged, so had my arousal." —Teresa M.

----

23 Ways to Shorten the Lesbian Sexual Rejuvenation Phase:

1. Do not break wind in bed, ever. Do use the bathroom for release of all noxious fumes.
2. Do have good dental hygiene. Do not brush or floss in front of your partner.
3. Do forego the onions, especially raw ones.
4. Use Beano.
5. After sex, do not ask for a performance evaluation (pathetic).
6. After sex, give glowing performance evaluations (generous).
7. Tell your partner what turns you on about her.
8. Don't process in bed.
9. Keep pets off the bed, especially during sex.
10. Don't panic! Be willing to wait out a lull, *without sniping.*
11. Don't threaten to go "outside the relationship" to get your needs met.

Leslie Lange

12. Don't nag.

13. Avoid passive-aggressive maneuvers, such as leaving your shoes on in bed.

14. See people! Go out! Get some fresh air for chrissake!

15. Keep things fresh. Throw away anything that reminds you of death or decay: old flowers, spoiled leftovers, photos of your grandparents.

16. Hire a feng shui practitioner to assess your home. The addition of a properly placed water element can be just the thing to get your libido going again.

17. Exercise, but don't exhaust yourself.

18. Take gingko, ginseng, or other placebos.

19. Run around the house naked singing opera music (this is a must).

20. Rearrange the furniture.

21. Change your hairstyle.

22. Wear a disguise.

23. Whatever you do, don't call it bed death. Remember, it's the "lesbian sexual rejuvenation phase."

Review: What Is Lesbian Bed Death?

• a condition in which lesbian couples simply stop having sex, characterized by a feeling of repulsion about one's partner that arises out of obsessing over (and magnifying) whatever's gross about her

• a period of sexual hibernation that occurs after the thrilling but exhausting lesbian romance phase

• a stigma invented by "the man" (a.k.a. the capitalist patriarchal establishment) to make dykes feel bad about themselves and discourage wives from dumping their husbands for grass-is-greener orgasms

- the same thing that happens when little children, and sometimes adults, gorge themselves on Halloween candy (a metaphor, folks!). Children love candy, but when they can have all they want it doesn't take long for the mere thought of candy to make them ill. After some time passes, candy starts to have an appeal again but is approached differently now, with a certain wisdom and caution that was not there to begin with. And that's a good thing. Remember when Mr. Rogers would sing about how learning is a good thing? Sometimes it's hard. Sometimes it's confusing. But still, it's a good thing.

The Closeted Relationship

The closet is a very lonely place. I was once so closeted I carried cedar chips in my pockets to keep moths from laying eggs all over me. Parties were very awkward, because I always stood facing sideways to other people. Once a cute dyke came up behind me and very sensuously adjusted my collar. "Hey," she said. "Your hanger's sticking out." So believe me, I know: The closet is not fun. Being in a relationship with someone in the closet is even less fun.

First of all, your girlfriend is not your girlfriend but your "roommate." If she holds your hand at the movies at all, she drops a sweater (or a leather jacket) over her lap first, then slithers her clammy hand into yours underneath it. She plays furtive footsie in restaurants and loves a good surprise make-out session—but only if the two of you are in an empty elevator. She's fanatical about curtains and window shades, which must always be drawn, even for a quick kiss or hug. She de-gays the house when her parents come to visit. She will not go with you to the Michigan Womyn's Music Festival.

Lesbian novelist Therese Szymanski once had the pleasure of being J's "roommate." Because J once had a fiancé she had even more evidence that Therese was really only a platonic buddy. When J's sister was about to get married and the couple was at J's mother's place, as they were leaving, the sister yelled across the house, "Should I send Therese her own invitation (to the wedding), or will she just come with you?" Even if this shock of exposure *had* given J a full-on cardiac arrest, no one would have known it because she never would have allowed herself to show an ounce of discomfort until she was safely alone. She could have died on the spot and kept walking and pretending everything was perfectly hetero-dandy. That's how closeted she was.

If you're in a relationship with a closeted woman, ultimately you'll have to decide for yourself how much you're willing to put up with and if you believe, over time, your partner will eventually be able to come out. Otherwise your life will be a living hell filled with shame, lies, and deception.

"My ex, Sharon, was never totally out. I felt like, since she's African-American and Southern, there was a lot of pressure on her from her family and from our extremely white college to stay in the closet. To me, her being butch was as plain as day, but for other people maybe it wasn't."
—Bridget C.

Dyke Drama

The Lesbian Predator and Dyke Relationships

Like a tramp's mascara, the label "predator" gets applied much too heavily in the lesbian community. A dyke can get branded a sociopath easier than she can find a decent job these days. As with most dyke drama, the drama of lesbian predators is blown way out of proportion. It's all part of the fun! If a dyke has an affair with half of a couple, she's a "homewrecker." If she sleeps with several dykes within the same peer group, she's "trouble." If she schemes and plots and calculates her way into the beds of lesbian after lesbian, she's a "UPS woman."

Most women who find themselves so labeled aren't really predators in a true sociopathic sense. They're just stuck with the lesbian community's strong need to produce symbolic villains. We need to believe in predators. If there are no bad lesbians, how will we reassure ourselves that we're good ones? But at whose expense are we doing this? Is the commitmentphobe truly a predator? Does she intentionally hurt other women? Or is she just another victim of her own good looks and charm? Maybe she's merely an accommodating young woman who has trouble saying no.

Sociopath or no sociopath, there are certain dykes who wreak havoc in the lesbian community. One sort is the gal who is solely attracted to women who are already in relationships. Why does she do this? Maybe she's unable to resist the appeal of the taboo. Perhaps she's afraid to face the challenges of a real relationship, so she develops a powerful fantasy: "I'd be so much better for Betty (or Kymbal or Scout) than her current partner." We call this hopeful daydreamer the Fantasy Monger.

The Fantasy Monger

Afraid of developing a true commitment with someone, this woman focuses her energy on impossible situations, preferring to exist in a fantasy relationship. While these Fantasy Mongers are often labeled predators, they're merely mired in psychological baggage. Still, this kind of dyke can sometimes successfully insinuate herself into a couple's lives under the guise of the "new best friend" or "margarita buddy," using a common interest she shares with one half of a particular couple to spend time with her envisioned future soul mate.

The Fantasy Monger has an entirely developed vision of how her fantasy relationship will play out, going as far as to imagine how many kids they will have and the brand of scented candles they'll use near the porcelain claw-foot tub in their future love nest. Her utopian vision is so intoxicating she forgets not only the pain of being perpetually single but also that it's bad form to hope for the dissolution of a healthy relationship. *Relationship?* she might think to herself when called out by her conscience. *What relationship?*

On one hand, it's your right to confront your partner and let her know exactly what you think is going on and what your feelings are. You'd like to order her to stop spending time with this she-devil, but such demands will only cause resentment. As your partner falls under her spell, you become acutely aware of this other woman's fantasy life. It makes you angry. How can your partner be so in denial? Well, she has good reason to be in denial: She doesn't want to give up this wonderful new friendship or whatever else the Fantasy Monger strings her along with. You start to feel like you're in the middle, in a sort of "no-dyke's-land." You're thrust into the position of having to trust your partner, and if you don't, she may say, "You're the one who's damaging this relationship! Your hysterical mistrust...your jealous inability to allow me to have other friends, etc." But if you *do* trust your partner, and she *does* wind up betraying you, what do you do then? "My first ex had an affair behind my back," remembers Beverly. "When I finally confronted her about it she said, 'It hasn't been going on long. *It's been less than a year.*' And I thought they'd just hooked up that weekend!"

It's certainly no fun to sit by helplessly and watch this happen. The best way to alleviate or neutralize the situation is to confront your partner with your feelings in a nonthreatening manner. Prepare yourself however you need to: Meditate or write out a script for yourself beforehand, whatever you can do to keep your tone as mellow and unperturbed as possible. Make yourself appear the "better choice." You are, after all. If you fly into hysterics, you may rightly be perceived as, well, hysterical. Breaking dishes against the wall will only make the other woman look more rational. Psychologically, the Fantasy Monger has an edge: It's not *her* relationship that's being threatened. When confronting a partner, it's essential to acknowledge the benefits she gets from being around this woman, but you must also express your worst suspicions, however silly they may seem. At all costs, you must remain your partner's ally. If the Fantasy Monger evolves into a stalker, you'll need each other for support.

To Escalate an Already Bad Situation:

• Go out of your way to make sure your lover and this woman are rarely alone together. Feign appendicitis if you have to. Or have a genuine attack. To induce appendicitis or other life-threatening intestinal problem, simply consume four cups of cooked day-old white rice in one sitting, deny yourself water, and wait 24 hours.

- Try to seduce the Fantasy Monger for yourself. Take her down, basically. Congratulations! You've just arranged for the implosion of your current relationship.

- Go into insane fits of rage each time the woman calls and point accusatory fingers in all directions. Shatter your favorite family heirloom as a symbol of self-sacrifice.

- Take it upon yourself to subtly—or not so subtly—threaten this woman. While this may seem a logical and morally justifiable step (as well as a hugely enjoyable one), it will no doubt backfire—she'll feel acknowledged as a peer and a viable competitor, and it will give her more power.

- Spy on them. Or get one of your equally fucked-up friends to do it.

- Hack into your lover's e-mail account in search of love notes or instant-message records.

- Make it known through your network of friends that this woman is trying to steal your girlfriend so that you turn her into a community pariah and make her life miserable.

It's normal for all these ideas to occur to a dyke caught in this dilemma. Yet if she acts on them, all are likely to backfire.

The Lesbian Lothario

Another misnamed predator is the Lesbian Lothario—a woman who becomes involved in a relationship while insisting on maintaining her "freedom." The L.L. manifests herself in various guises: "lone wolf," "misunderstood artist," "playa," "horizon opener," and "intellectual."

Acclaimed author and Class IV dyke drama survivor Jewelle Gomez thought she'd found the perfect partner, but after a short period during which tiny cupids swam continually about her head, she realized her lover was "compulsively non-monogamous." Gomez elaborated: "Under the guise of personal freedom she avoided commitment like it was a communicable disease." As Gomez hung in there, life became more difficult. "On the very first trip we took together we were surrounded by women she'd either slept with in the past or had promised to sleep with in the future. All smirking at me. She was writing postcards to a potential conquest during our vacation. When a conquest got to be too much for her, or boring, she'd drop her—and then I had to answer the telephone whenever one of them called!"

But it would be a mistake to label this kind of Sapphic seducer as malicious; she's more like a fanatical hobbyist. Still, if you're a monogamous girl, life with Lothario is not much fun. She sure puts you in an awkward position. She's smart, gritty. She has a viable personal philosophy: Sexual abundance is natural and good. She can back up her philosophy by citing various political and literary allies—her favorites being warty old Jean-Paul Sartre and Simone de Beauvoir, and the adored Frida Kahlo and Diego Rivera.

It's possible that the sorts of people who successfully employ this sexual philosophy are less common, perhaps more intellectual than most, perhaps more evolved. It's also possible that the L.L.'s sophistication is a charade to lure her monogamous partner into compliance. Whatever the truth, no Lesbian Lothario is so evolved that she avoids tiresome drama. Take Lillian's story, for example:

> Possibly the toughest situation is to date two people (women) at once. I did it, and it lasted about three

months before imploding. I had just asked my girlfriend (code name "A") of three years to move out because I wasn't sure I wanted to continue the relationship into the distant future. We didn't break up then—we continued to see each other but with the understanding that it would no longer necessarily be an exclusive relationship. She moved into her own place a few blocks away from me. At the same time another woman (code name "B") came along, and since I was attracted to her and I was no longer in a monogamous-type situation, I began dating her. She happened to live in the exact same neighborhood. All three of us rented apartments in about a five-block-square area.

I was honest with both and they each knew about the other and had met the other socially. Problem number 1 was that their phone numbers were EXACTLY THE SAME EXCEPT FOR THE LAST DIGIT.

Problem number 2 was that every second I wasn't around, each assumed I was having hot sex with the other one. So each of them wanted to know where I was at all times, questioned me as to who I'd been with last night, who I'd been with at lunch, who I'd been with, who, who, who. Each would get angry if she thought I was spending too much time with the other. And every second I was out of sight I was spending too much time with the other. Also, for all they knew, I was dating dozens more women on the sly. This they found upsetting.

Problem number 3 was that since A and B were both women, I couldn't easily distinguish among their personal effects. One day I found a pair of earrings on the bedside table and later handed them to A, saying

"You left these here." She gave me a look that would shrivel a coconut and said, "These aren't mine." That was the beginning of the end.

The final analysis was that it was impossible for me to manage all the fiery emotions swirling around my apartment and neighborhood. One way or another, we all broke it off and started over with new girlfriends.

My friend Beatrice refused to be monogamous in any of her many relationships until age 36. She found that while she could choose her philosophy, she could not choose whom she would fall for. Invariably, they all were looking for monogamy. The beautiful and charming Beatrice had an easy time finding women who were willing to compromise—but their willingness waned once the passion wore off.

Beatrice found that while she wanted to have her "freedom" she could not shrug off her emotional attachments to all the trust-funded Vassar grads whose fuzzy cups had been so fun to sip at. After nine or ten torrential relationships lasting a maximum of two years apiece, the steady pattern of love and loss took its toll and she turned a complete about-face: She became so conservative we now have to restrain her in a strait-jacket whenever the Log Cabin Republicans come to town.

"It's something perhaps gay men do better...I don't know. I can't say non-monogamy isn't right for some people; it was certainly for me when I was younger. Although I personally put lots of women through hell, I was always ethical about it, always honest and upfront. That didn't stop me from becoming a pariah. Let's just say I was unwelcome in certain circles. Women would literally turn their backs on me at parties...." —anonymous Lesbian Lothario in recovery (duh, it's Beatrice!)

It seems a simple case of logic: If you're a woman who wishes to be nonmonogamous, it's wise to steer clear of those who are seeking monogamy. Conversely, if you're seeking a monogamous relationship, don't cling to a woman who wants to be free. Yet these two types of women, the settle-downers and run-arounders, latch on to each other—*thwock! thwock! thwock!*—like magnets to a refrigerator.

"You gotta think about that," said Beatrice. "I sure had to. Why was I so attracted, why did I feel I had so much more in common with these humdrum monogamists? Why didn't I want to be with that polyamorous blue-haired girl with the bone in her nose? I've sort of danced around couples who were polyamorous. There was jealousy, always jealousy. It would always be like: 'Yeah, well, we have an open relationship, but when you pick me up, don't come to the door, because Susie gets jealous.' "

The bottom line: If you're nonmonogamous because you don't want to jump through hoops for people, the reality is that you may wind up jumping through even more hoops than you would if you were monogamous. It takes weeks of haggling—not to mention hours mulling over hurt feelings, jealousies, and the like—just to come up with a set of basic rules both parties can agree on.

Sample guidelines for managing nonmonogamy appear in D. Merilee Clunis and G. Dorsey Green's *Lesbian Couples: A Guide to Creating Healthy Relationships*. When laying out rules, you and your partner should decide whether outside affairs should:

- be kept a secret
- be discussed
- not take place with mutual friends
- only occur with anonymous partners

- only occur when one partner is out of town
- not take place at home or in the couple's bedroom
- only take place as a threesome involving both partners

Once a set of poly guidelines is established for a couple, you can both relax in the knowledge that while rules can be restrictive, they are also meant to be broken. And now you've just come up with a whole slew of them to choose from. "How may I betray you?" asks the nonmonogamous partner. "Let me count the ways."

"It's all supposed to be about sexual freedom," Beatrice groaned, "but this freedom costs you much more freedom—in the way of time, effort, and heartache—than your lack of it."

The Sologamist

The "sologamist" (author's terminology) is a sort of faux nonmonogamist. Often trapped in an insular lesbian community, the sologamist is the lesbian no one will date. Maybe her insistence on having multiple partners has gotten her blacklisted. Maybe her charms have faded. Whatever the reason, she's having a stretch of bad luck and no one's biting. The nonmonogamous "sologamist" may resort to leaving town just to rediscover her mojo.

Monogamy Righteousness

Usually found in those who are monogamous, not because they choose to be but because they fear sexuality in general. It's easy to recognize. Look for the woman who's speaking about nonmonogamous women with utter disdain, who uses words like "whore" and "gross." She often also thinks penises are "disgusting."

Righteous monogamists are in danger of becoming righteous

vegetarians, righteous fitness freaks (a.k.a. the evil "no carbs" lesbian), and righteous pains in the ass. They are often serious lesbians, or just stunted. Note to the righteous: Treat nonmons with the courtesy you'd like for yourself. If you happen to run into one on a blind date, offer to hook her up with other nonmons you know. She'll never forget the favor.

"Helpful, not hurtful" is the motto for you.

The Drama Couple

"My friend and her lover would beat each other up and then make up. It was a kind of sick game they played. Also, the lover would threaten suicide every time my friend wanted to break up. The lover would call her when she was out to tell her she had to come home right away or she would kill herself." —Jenny, former victim of a dyke-drama couple

The dyke-drama couple is usually a very attractive couple, very social, very much a part of the "in" crowd. They've been together "forever"—in a way that's become mythical to their insular circle of lesbian friends. (These friends continually argue, with equal numbers in both camps, over which one in the couple is more beautiful.) They're like local celebrities: fun, flirtatious, colorful. Their glamour inspires fellow dykes.

The drama couple has everything. But they need something more. In fact, the only thing—the one thing!—that keeps their relationship going is the presence of drama. They need drama to thrive, to define their love. It's the glue that holds them together, the gaudy glitter of their charisma.

Beware, my dears: The drama couple is toxic.

How do they get this drama they need? One way is to bring in, by way of seduction, a third party. The sales pitch will often go like this: "Judy cheated on me, and she still lies about it, and

I've never really gotten over it, and now I think she's cheating on me again, but there's nothing I can do because I'm financially dependent on her, and...well, I stopped loving her a long time ago, but there's no use..." and so on. The usually fun and flirty woman tells horror story after horror story ("Michelle has a terrible temper, but no one knows...") and professes to be "miserable." The poor wretch who is smitten with her sees this as a sign that the relationship is ending. She sees herself as rescuing a beautiful beleaguered princess.

Nothing could be further from the truth. In fact, as long as the drama continues, this couple's relationship is ROCK SOLID. They will almost always fall back on each other, realizing at the end of each destructive episode how much they really loved each other all along. This scenario can play out in the course of a single evening—or it may take several months. Smoky bars and sexually charged lesbian barbecues provide the ideal environment. While tending bar, lesbian novelist Therese Szymanski saw the same scenario night after night: "They get drunk, the femme flirts and tries to bring in an unsuspecting butch, so her butch can go all rooster and try to stake her claim."

L Word superfemmes Marina and Francesca are the Los Angeles lipstick version of the dyke-drama couple. Marina seduces the overwhelmed Jenny, neglecting to clue her in about Francesca until after Jenny splits from her long-term boyfriend. When Francesca returns from an overseas trip she asserts her presence back into the relationship, telling Jenny "while I'm in town, I like to have her to myself." Jenny throws a fit. On her way to the car, she turns and hurls a bottle of wine at their house (thrown bottles of alcohol count as Class IV dyke drama). Days later she recounts the story for a gang of punchy lesbians at the Dinah Shore golf tournament, thus completing the cycle of drama by giving it back to the community in the form of lesbian oral history.

Leslie Lange

The dyke-drama couple weaves a web that exaggerates the normal drama occurring between them. This web is used to snare other lesbians.

--------------------------------✐◻--------------------------------

True Testimonial:
One Lesbian's Terrible Triangle

"When I was just nineteen, I got sucked in by this tall, beautiful couple. I'll call them Arachna and Melissa. Each worked on seducing me at the same time. I found myself in an awkward night of three-way sex that led to my sneaking around with Arachna, an olive-skinned Armenian with a very real-looking tattoo of a black widow spider lowering itself into her bush. One day, Arachna told me she would leave Melissa. The next day, the two held a huge shouting match in a public park near our apartment complex, and the next day they were back together, professing to be more in love than ever before. · Years later they were still running the same program, with young baby dykes fresh out of high school as their latest conquests." —anonymous in Michigan

--------------------------------❦--------------------------------

Rules to Navigate the Drama Couple's Web

• As a principle, always assume that falling in love with one half (or both halves) of a drama couple ensures the couple's continued existence.

• The only way for these couples to break up is if nobody ever gets sucked in and they're forced to hash out their problems in a vacuum.

• If you do succumb to an affair, expect one of three things to happen:

1. Your affair will cause a huge uproar that will alienate you from this woman and her partner, and possibly an entire

posse of lesbian friends (depending on how enmeshed the group is).

2. You may receive threats from or become involved in a physical altercation with the woman's lover. This includes the possibility of being present for an embarrassing public confrontation and/or possible visitation in the workplace. Remember, LESBIANS ARE CAPABLE OF ANYTHING, so watch out.

3. If on the odd chance you succeed in breaking up this relationship, you're guaranteed plenty of drama with the ex; and within a few years or less, you'll be on the other end of this woman's whining and complaining to the next hot chick who comes along.

How to Avoid the Web of the Dyke-Drama Couple
Establish a policy of unavailability.

Self-statement: I am not a sounding board for this woman's relationship problems, especially when there's this weird sexual tension. While I may tell myself I'm only being a good listener or a good friend, what I'm really doing is letting myself be seduced.

The more you hear about this woman's horrible partner, the more you want to hear, and the more you start to see yourself taking her place. If you hear yourself thinking or saying, "Oh, I would never..." you're putting yourself in that frame of mind— of actually being able to justify cheating, to justify participating in a deception. (This isn't the same as sleeping with someone in an open relationship.) If she's enticing you into a deception by complaining about her lover, the best thing to do is stop her in her tracks: Change the subject. Set a limit. Make an excuse to leave. Whatever you do, don't reinforce the "poor me" kind of complaining that goes on. It's bad manners when you think about it: to complain to a lesbian friend about one's lover (especially to a new friend). We have old friends—and exes—for that kind of thing.

Are You Part of a Dyke-Drama Couple?

1. Do you find your sex life perking up when there's a flirtation with another woman?
2. Have you ever acted on a flirtation, then ran back to your current lover to have jealousy-fueled make-up sex?
3. Are public temper tantrums common in your relationship? Are they a type of foreplay?
4. Are you a diss queen? Do you trash your partner to women you're attracted to?
5. Does your name end in "a"—as in Theresa, Karina, Rita, or Martina?

Newcomer Phenomenon

So, what to do when your partner starts a friendship with a new lesbian? Does she make a point of seeing her all by herself, excluding you on their special excursions to play Scrabble and gossip at the local coffee shop? Moreover, what if the newcomer's one of those "straight but curious" gals?—she's aching to come out, and you've seen the way she goes all moony-eyed around your girl. Your girlfriend tells you she's "just being nice to her" and grows misty about the good old days when *she* was coming out and also had no one to talk to... "It's therapeutic," she tells you. "I'm nurturing old wounds."

Regardless of the reality, your mind goes off on its own. You can't get things done because you're too busy worrying: *Is she really an innocent friend? Or is Ruth just using her as a lever to get out of her relationship with me? Why is Ruth always so happy when she gets back from those stupid Scrabble tournaments?* Relax—jealousy is normal; you wouldn't feel it if you didn't care. But remember, jealousy can be as irrational as it is irritating; like a religious fervor, it can escalate into all sorts of rude behavior, such as crouching behind the Dumpster in back of the local lesbian coffee shop with a loaded semiautomatic paintball gun.

The best way to handle a threatening newcomer is to calmly let your feelings be known *to your partner* at the most neutral time you can find. This does not mean (as it did for an acquaintance of mine) spiking her drinks with Vicodin then interrogating her about her perceived infidelity. Setting an appointment to talk about something "important" is a nice way to go about it. Your partner is less likely to feel encroached upon, she'll sweat bullets wondering what it's all about in the meantime, and by the time the two of you sit down to talk you'll have her full attention. Whatever you do, control all urges to make sly barbs (no matter how clever) or sling passive-aggressive comments at her. Do not spy or otherwise invade your partner's privacy. Do not verbally accost the "other woman" at her home or place of work. Do not physically accost her in these places either. If you catch her alone in a dark alley, you are not—as some believe—"home free."

Queer scholar Justine Moss believes that working through her feelings with her partner on the advent of a threatening newcomer was an excellent trust builder. "If your girlfriend does screw you over," Moss says, "remember this: She's the fool. Move on—you're better off in the long run."

Domestic Violence

What's hard about lesbian domestic violence is admitting it, sort of like when you just bought a lemon of a used car. Once I traded in my perfectly good Honda Civic for a hot looking Mazda RX7 with no warranty and the damn thing broke down within a month. I was so ashamed I couldn't tell anyone. In the same way, more than once I thought I was getting a good deal by swapping a life of patriarchal oppression for a life of matriarchal oppression. Nobody warned me about the latter. I was even more ashamed and definitely couldn't tell anyone.

If you're in an abusive situation, please, by all means, get help. Enlist your friends, family, or social workers. If necessary, contact the police. The worst thing you can do to yourself is stay in an abusive environment, no matter how much you "care" about your abuser.

Couples Counseling:
Bourgeois Solution vs. Big Fat Rip-Off

My wife is fond of suggesting that since I'm the one with all the problems we'd save money on couples counseling by just sending *me* to therapy. I'm fond of suggesting that this type of attitude is exactly why we need to be in couples counseling in the first place, but let's face it: Couples counseling is really, really expensive. It's nearly twice as expensive as regular counseling, although it's no more labor intensive. I've done both, and in each type the practitioner sits placidly in her chair for the entire hour. I mean, what is that about? Who do these therapists think they're kidding? What are they charging so much for? Is there a rental fee on sofa space? Oxygen consumption? Perhaps therapists are very sensitive to oxygen-level shifts in the room and treating two people threatens their comfort zone. Don't these therapists ever get out?

OK, so there's a lot more for a therapist to contend with in the way of hysteria and people shouting at each other. But by that rationale, therapy should be more expensive for angry people who shout at their therapists—but it isn't, is it?

What can we do? They've got us over a barrel.

There are all sorts of excuses *not* to go to couples counseling. But for those of us who struggle under such factors as abysmal economic status; social isolation due to stereotypically bad fashion sense signaled by mullet hairstyles, bolo ties, and drawstring surfer pants; a tendency toward alcohol and other substance abuse; and a propensity for internalized-anger syndromes, couples therapy can be a substitute for what everyday society provides to straight couples for free: mentoring, a set of guidelines for success, affirmation of the relationship, and a safe space to explore all the crap behind the conflict. (Some lesbians will only seek counseling if their relationship troubles escalate to the point of physical abuse. News flash: Once your troubles have escalated to the point of physical abuse, the most helpful solution is to get the hell out. Research has shown that while batterers may stop hitting their partners, they continue to psychologically manipulate them. And who wants that?)

The scary thing about couples counseling is that one dyke is always there to point out the other's hypocrisy—commonly known as "calling her on her shit." The same thing happens on *Judge Judy.* After a spate of heated interruptions, followed by "Maxine's a lying bitch!" the therapist finally slams down the gavel, shouting, "Order! Order!" She firmly gains control and facilitates a novel "taking turns" approach to the dialogue. Adriane tells her side of the story while Maxine sits with her arms folded, shaking her head, as if it were all more than a saint could bear. When it's Maxine's turn to talk, Adriane clears her throat loudly at each new arrival of bullshit. These are the beginnings of "healthy communication."

Finding the Perfect Therapist

Though it's hard to find a good therapist, this should never be a reason to use one partner's individual therapist for couples therapy. Psychologists are trained to be impartial, but they're still human beings. The saintly Dr. Helen, who's listened nonjudgmentally to your partner's lopsided version of the truth for months on end, may have a bone to pick with you when you show up. One woman told me about how she once brought her partner in to have a "co-session" with her shrink of five years. "I don't know what happened—maybe she suddenly grasped what a weak, pathetic person I was with—but my therapist just snapped. It was ugly. She totally trashed Lisa, reduced her to a mass of tears."

Even if you do choose someone who knows nothing about either of you, there's no guarantee she'll be bias-free. "I went to a lesbian couples therapist with my girlfriend," said Tina S., "and the therapist developed a crush on me, agreed with everything I said, and at one point told my girlfriend to 'shut up.' Needless to say, that was the end of the therapy."

A good couples therapist will (a) enable each angry lesbian to see her own part in whatever conflicts need to be resolved; (b) provide a safe place to explore challenging issues; (c) have some experience being in a couple his or herself; and (d) likely charge an arm and a leg.

A bad couples therapist will (a) violate confidentiality; (b) develop a crush on one or the other of you and consciously or unconsciously plot your relationship's demise to suit her own desires; (c) extend the frequency and duration of your sessions just to make a buck; or (d) explore her own lesbian desires through you.

Willingness to work on a sliding scale is an indication of neither a bad nor a good therapist.

Almost every dyke has a therapist horror story or two in her arsenal, and couples counselors are no exception. "I once went to this therapist with my girlfriend, Liz," said Amy C. from Las Vegas. "We were in the middle of breaking up and probably just couldn't admit it to ourselves. The therapist was listed in the *Gay and Lesbian Yellow Pages* as 'specializing in gay and lesbian relationships.' However, on our first visit, she informed us that she was straight. She was very loquacious, a former dancer, and often distracted by whimsical thoughts. In the middle of one session, she stared intensely at Liz and blurted. 'Have you had a nose job?'

" 'No,' said Liz. 'Why?'

" 'Well,' she chuckled. 'You wouldn't have to tell me if you did.'

" 'Well, I didn't,' said Liz.

" 'It's just that you have the most perfect nose,' said the therapist. 'It's like a little Cupid's nose.'

"In the same session she wound up talking about what a difficult time lesbians have breaking up, and she used as an example a couple she'd been counseling and how she'd finally gotten them to move on when all of a sudden one day she got a phone call from 'Louise,' who said, 'Laura and I don't need to come in anymore. We've realized how much we love each other, so we're moving back in together and we're going to be together forever.' The therapist paused to roll her eyes. 'And I just thought, *Oh, sure...they have a really sick relationship.*'

"Sure, it was off-the-wall, but at the time we didn't think too much of it—other than joking with each other in the car that maybe she was on a mission to break up as many lesbian couples as she could—until a couple of sessions later, when I made a joke about Liz and I being like the proverbial Laura and Louise. Well, the therapist just suddenly sat up in her chair. 'Oh, my God!' she said. 'You know Laura and Louise?!'

"Liz and I just looked at each other. She hadn't even bothered to change the names..."

Tips for Successful Couples Therapy

- Minimize your commute time to and from therapy to avoid driving home together in reckless anger.
- Don't stick with a wacky therapist, such as one who eats lunch during the session, bangs a little gong to signal the beginning and end of each session, or seems overly interested in acting as a sexual surrogate for either or both of you.
- Unless you're a masochist (or a total idiot), never use one partner's primary therapist for couples counseling
- Go Dutch when it comes to payment, or alternate who pays. Do not try to save a buck by making sure the last visit ends on her tab, not yours.
- Don't act like a Jerry Springer guest if you find out she's been cheating. It may bias the therapist against you in the future.
- Storming out of the session is sometimes a "healthy" demonstration of anger. To prevent humiliation, remember to grab your car keys on the way out.

Family Planning

As more and more dykes stampede hell-bent and lemming-like to the sperm bank, drama in and around getting pregnant is now the 13th biggest reported problem in the lesbian community. (That might seem sort of down there on the list, but this is out of the billions of problems reported every year.)

The Traitor Inseminator

"You're not going to believe what happened to my friend Paula," Carrie M. in Seattle told me. "She and her girlfriend decided to have a child. They went to this lesbian feminist clinic and found a great doctor who was, you know, really helpful through the entire process: sperm selection, timing the cycle, and so on. During the insemination, the doctor was talking to Paula's girlfriend in this low throaty voice, and there was this palpable sort of...sexual tension. Of course it seemed weird—her girlfriend's legs were quivering in the stirrups—but she put it out of her mind. Six weeks into her girlfriend's pregnancy, she left Paula for the woman who inseminated her. Talk about a scandal!"

IKEA Syndrome

It's amazing, isn't it, how a perfectly loving couple can begin to feel murderous toward each other just by collaborating to assemble a Bojnüs cabinet from IKEA? Well, guess what? Collaborating on a baby is 30 times worse. There are even more unfamiliar-looking components, the instructions are jargonistic and practically indecipherable, and it takes months, sometimes years, to get it right. This holds true for the paperwork requirements for adoption and the complex physical steps necessary to assure the biological participation of both mothers.

"I hear them screaming day and night," says Rene J. who lives next door to a would-be couple of lesbian moms. "No, Denise, the egg goes into a test tube first, then gets the sperm, then it goes into me!"

"But I'm sure the doctor said the egg goes into you first, then the sperm gets added..."

"No, no, no!!! I don't want to talk about it anymore. We'll ask the doctor again next time we see her."

Leslie Lange

"Oh, great. You don't want to talk about it because you know I'm right!"

"That is such bullshit!"

And so on.

I say, anybody who can pass this test is way smarter than most people.

Baby-Making Quiz*

See if you can put the words below into a sentence that actually makes sense and leads to lesbian motherhood.

**doctor • sperm in a can • anonymous donor
fertilized egg • underwater birthing tank
test tube • lab • egg of partner 1 • midwife
uterus of partner 2 • embryo
hospital • baby**

Answer: The **egg of partner 1** is gathered by the **doctor.** The egg is fertilized in the **lab** in a **test tube** by **sperm in a can** from an **anonymous donor.** The **fertilized egg** is then implanted into the **uterus of partner 2.** Partner 2 carries the **embryo** as it develops into a **baby,** which is born at home in an **underwater birthing tank** with the assistance of a **midwife**—unless there's a serious complication during labor, in which case the baby may be delivered in a **hospital.***

----

*Please feel free to copy this answer and keep in your wallet in times of need.

Dyke Drama

The Final Word:
Tips for Healthy Lesbian Relationships

- Never skip a meal in favor of processing (or sex).
- Take whatever measures are necessary to avoid Double PMS.
- Wait till you've seen your lover's dark side before you move in together.
- Stay in touch with friends. You'll need them.
- Do not covet thy neighbor's wife.
- Practice judicious use of couples counseling at any stage of the relationship.
- When starting a family, beware of the traitor inseminator.

Leslie Lange

The Drama of
The Drama of
LESBIAN SEX

sex as folklore
* the drama of pets
and lesbian sex * why can't
s/m and vanilla get along? *
monogamy schmonogamy
* interview with a pillow princess
dyke sex cyberdrama * sex addiction
* lesbian sex clubs: proof or spoof? *
dangerous lesbians * burning up for your
love * freeway to a three-way

"Some girls go from kissing to rubbing on your leg like a bunny in heat. There are many of these women. They frighten me. There's a difference between the good old bump and grind and having your leg humped." —Bett W.

Never underestimate the power of sex, which has built and obliterated families, nations, and food co-ops. Along the continuum of sexual expression, the number of possible variations is infinite. This translates to an infinite number of things lesbians can find to disapprove of. Never underestimate the capacity of lesbians, especially serious lesbians, to insist there is only one right way to do anything.

"That isn't politically correct" was once a favorite phrase. But one rarely hears it anymore. Instead it floats silently in the air because, beyond the clucking church ladies of the world, beyond the raised eyebrows of elementary school librarians, serious lesbians have perfected the art of nonverbal disapproval. They have honed the hiss, groomed the gas-face, perfected the pompous snort. Gay men may be the queens of diss, but lesbians are crueler in silence—especially about sex.

Sex as Folklore

Despite a propensity for judging sexual behavior, some dykes are pretty free with information-sharing. Nothing beats the dramatic potential of a good lesbian sex story. For one thing, we're renowned for our props. Sure, boys have us beat in sheer numbers, but trips to the ER for removal of imaginative insertables are not an exclusive occurrence. Mishaps with homemade sex implements—such as dark-chocolate-filled Easter eggs whose shells break apart inside the vagina, or the infamous condom-covered electric toothbrush—may cause embarrassing injuries to one's private area, but it's nothing a little aloe vera or calendula oil won't cure.

Sometimes a sex story reveals more about the teller (like how much she'll put up with): "I once dated a girl who liked to sleep in the nude," said one woman. "Her dog slept in the bed as well. Sure, it was nothing sexual, but it *was* itchy, and it *was* stinky. Yuck!" But the best stories are deeply personal and weird. For example:

"My ex could only get off in an extremely specific rhythm that is nearly impossible to replicate without a jackhammer. She also fashioned dildos for herself out of melted candles (she grew up in the Middle East, so she didn't have much choice). It freaked me out when I first found them, but in the grand scheme of things, it's not that strange." —Bridget C.

"I dated one girl who was really slight in stature, and then we got into the bedroom. She asked me to 'make love' to her with her favorite dildo. She pulled this puppy out and, oh, my God—I swear to you, I thought it was a small building. This thing was wrapped

in velvet, tucked away, and huge. I just couldn't believe what this shy woman wanted. It was quite the eye-opener." —Arden

Not all involve dildos:

"One time my girlfriend and I had a three-way with this chick who had a yeast infection. She didn't seem to be aware of this. We didn't want to hurt her feelings, so one of us had to 'go there.' I was the heroic one who leapt on the grenade. I still haven't quite recovered." —Bett W.

"My friend Angela has a notched labia from when her girl-friend got a little sloppy with the razor." —Diana Cage, in the book *Box Lunch*

And some are competitive:

"That summer we had sex in every bathroom stall at the Getty museum." —Lindsay W.

Many of our stories originate from the "when two worlds collide" phenomenon. "This girl in a dyke bar I met in a small city flipped out when she realized I was packing. She actually said the word *patriarchal.* Repeatedly," reports one woman.
"She pressed against me and it turned out she was packing!" reports another. "Can you believe it?"
Storytelling is important to our culture. To maintain a drama-free life, be discreet about identifying specific individuals, unless you're trying to tip off someone you think might enjoy a certain predilection—or warn someone about a potential hazard. I like to make up a fictional ex (a.k.a."the baby talker from hell") to whom I credit all the odd sexual behaviors of my current partner. Trust

me, she'll appreciate it. Don't reenact for a potluck audience the way your lover sounds when she's coming, but exes are open game. Before relaying a shocking experience, take a moment to ask yourself if this story reveals something about your own sexual prudishness, and be willing to accept the possibility that we're drawn to what shocks us most.

"I liked to have really rough sex, including hair pulling and smacking each other around. It freaked me out a little at first, until I realized she was responding to something I gave out and I realized how much I really liked to get hit during sex." —Bridget C.

With Dog as My Witness: The Drama of Pets and Lesbian Sex

Remember the woman whose lover let her dog stay on the bed during sex? ("Sure it was nothing sexual, but it *was* itchy, and it *was* stinky. Yuck!") She might count her blessings if she saw what else was out there. The following is derived from a passage entitled "Animals" from Pat Califia's *Sapphistry: The Book of Lesbian Sexuality,* published in 1980 by Naiad Press Inc.:

> Fantasies that include animals are very common. The sensual attraction of the animal plus the forbidden nature of the experience can make these fantasies very exciting. When it comes to reality, you may have trouble deciding whether you've ever had an experience with

bestiality. Does it turn you on to pet your collie? Do you have a cat that insists on lying on your chest while you masturbate? Some experiences with animals are more clearly sexual. Children often explore the genitals of the family pet or allow an animal to smell and lick their genitals. If you have a pet, you may massage its genitals when it comes into heat and can't be allowed to have sex with a member of its own species. You may allow your favorite animal to stay in the room while you masturbate or make love. Dogs become especially interested in sexual noises and smells and may want to taste sexual juices or perspiration on your skin and vulva without any encouragement from you.

Being sexual with animals can cause some anxiety, largely because of the threat of disapproval or ridicule. Other concerns can be dealt with more easily. If you are not compelling the animal to accept your attentions and you are gentle, you will not harm it emotionally or physically. Concerns about hygiene can be alleviated by washing yourself or your nonhuman, furry friend. Conception cannot occur as a result of sex between humans and animals of other species....

You need not choose between loving women and loving animals. The emotional and sexual content of these two experiences is very different. Women don't have fur, can't purr, and don't bother you to be walked every morning. Animals don't talk, earn their own livings, squeeze fresh orange juice, or write love poems.

This excerpt brings up several questions, first and foremost being: Was Califia on crack when she wrote this? And was her editor at Naiad also on crack? But also, if my girlfriend stopped talking to me, and never earned her own living, let alone squeezed a drop of fresh orange juice or wrote me a single love poem, can I get away with calling her a beast?

Fortunately, a lot has changed since the '80s. Other than the "open-minded" Califia passage, which I stumbled across while conducting actual research on lesbian sex practices, I was unable to find any lesbians who admitted to having sex with their animals (though a few avoided eye contact when they answered me). I did learn, however, that many lesbians do "allow" their beloved pets to remain on the bed.

"Sometimes our long-haired miniature dachshund, Cassandra, stays on the bed with us during sex. But only if she's sleeping and we're too lazy or caught up in the moment to bother with her. She just snores away through the whole process anyway, and she's so small she stays completely out of the way. But one time we rolled over and Cassandra was just sitting there, staring. We banished her to the floor immediately." —Tania L.

Wondering if your pet harbors a sexual crush on you, or whether one may ethically masturbate one's cat as long as it's in heat and can't mate with a member of its own species is really way beyond the scope of this study, my intellect, and everyone's sense of good taste. However, I promised myself at the onset of this project that as an author and a hack I had a duty not to shy away from putting something in for purely sensationalist purposes.

Now let's talk about the *real* dangers of keeping one's pets on the bed: extreme pet jealousy. If you think I'm joking, check out *When Pets Come Between Partners,* by Joel Gavriele-Gold (which talks about the "human-pet-human triangle"), or *If Only They Could Speak,* by animal behaviorist Nicholas Dodman. Let's face it: The pet-lesbian relationship is often codependent. For example, single lesbians, longing for companionship, isolated from their coupled friends, invest tremendous emotional energy in their pets.

Let's take the case of Allison B., who rescued a tick-covered, one-eyed terrier from the pound during a long single phase we refer to as "a sustained period of personal transformation." Freckles was a special-needs dog (making him a very special match for a special-needs lesbian). His one good eye required drops three times per day, a procedure he didn't like at all—as his snapping jaws so eloquently communicated. Gradually, Allison's patience and gentleness with the scruffy rascal won out. He transformed into a well-behaved charmer. Soon he settled into the happy routine of snuggling up at the foot of Allison's bed to sleep each night. His snapping jaws became a thing of the past, mentioned only as part of the mythology of his misfit phase, nothing like the sweet, tawny dog he was now.

Then Allison found a girlfriend.

Suddenly Freckles was no longer basking in the radiance of Allison's attention. He received fewer treats, fewer pats on the head, fewer rides in the car. Whereas Allison once loved to sit on the sofa and gaze at him for hours, she now gazed into space with sweet Katie on her mind. Freckles was left alone for longer stretches of time.

One night, early on, the new girlfriend was over and she and Allison were in the throes of some wild, naked tribadism. Tormented by the sounds he associated with the loss of his best friend, mother, and soul mate, Freckles slunk into the bedroom, hunkered low, and spied through his single, sharp, black eye the foot of the intruder, the usurper of his love! Freckles sprang. His jaws latched on to a soft, pink toe, and—in a terrier version of *Call of the Wild*—he dug in his fangs till he felt them hit bone. "It was horrible," said Allison, "like an oil geyser. The blood shot up and out."

To Prevent Attacks From Jealous Dogs:

- Give the dog a small amount of Benadryl (ask your vet for proper dosage instructions) and—as you would with a child—wait to have sex until the canine conks out. For added safety, and in case of regained consciousness, shut the dog out of any room you're about to get jiggy in. As an alternative, some animal behaviorists have had success with Prozac, which boosts doggie self-esteem.

- Shower the dog with affection, more than ever before. Ask a friend to baby-sit the dog when you go out on dates.

- This is harsh, but it can save lives. Use a muzzle to keep your lover from saying anything that might offend the dog.

Leslie Lange

Feline attacks are more difficult to address since most cats couldn't care less about what's happening between their owner and another person. They're much more concerned with issues of territory. Cats are also more likely to attack randomly, not just when their owner is having sex.

To Reduce Your Risk of a Cat Attack:

- Change the comforter cover or blanket on the bed.
- Introduce new furniture.
- Again, sometimes kitty Prozac does the trick.
- Get rid of the new lover. Cats have good instincts after all.

Avoid pet sex drama in general by keeping good sexual boundaries with pets. Critters can be crafty little voyeurs. Just because darling Boo Boo is snoring or has his gummy little eyes closed, it doesn't mean the conniving little eunuch isn't faking the funk just to cop a cheap thrill. Finally, and most importantly, please remember: There's a fine line between letting your cat on the bed and letting it camp on your chest when you masturbate. And it's a line that PETA does not want you to cross.

Note: In May 2004, I e-mailed PETA to ask if there was an official stance on the subject of "noncoercive sex with domesticated animals." In June 2004, they sent this reply:

```
Hello,
    Thank you for contacting PETA with your
concerns about the very serious issue of
bestiality, a crime involving humans' use
of animals for sexual pleasure.
```

A sexual interaction of an other-than-human animal by a human could never be considered consensual since the animal cannot truly consent. As an organization, we believe that animals do not belong to humans for our own uses, and using an animal for sexual gratification is a clear and dangerous example of human abuse of a relationship with an animal. An animal's sexuality—including humans—is only healthily and naturally expressed with another of its own species.

Bestiality is a highly abusive and exploitative form of assault and can be harmful or even deadly. We encourage everyone to take action against this violent crime.

I hope that you find this information helpful. Thanks so much for your compassion for animals.

Sincerely,
Jeff Mackey, Correspondent, People for the Ethical Treatment of Animals

Why Can't S/M and Vanilla Get Along?

Not since the cootie wars of kindergarten have two subgroups disdained each other more than vanilla and S/M lesbians. Heightened biases have never run higher.

According to the vanilla lesbians I've polled, S/M dykes: are deviants; are just trying to get attention; take themselves too seriously; are enemies of capitalism and of gay and lesbian equality; define themselves by their sexuality; and have a false superiority complex. Tops are secretly wimpy. Bottoms are narcissistic manipulators and usually major control freaks. S/M dykes are tattooed; wear leather; give decent, family-oriented lesbians a bad name; and take the joy out of sex by labeling everything with some sort of power dynamic. They're dismissive of us just because we're vanilla. They listen to Enigma. They think they're so cool and edgy and punk, and it's nothing but a front. They're antifeminist. They look at me like I'm dirt.

According to S/M dykes polled, vanilla lesbians: are a bunch of prudes who still wish straight people would love them; assume all those who practice S/M were abused as children; shop at J.Crew and Banana Republic; and are disgusted by the so-called cruelty of S/M but couldn't care less about child labor violations. They are "the man." Vanilla lesbians won't admit they have power dynamics too. Vanilla lesbians practice domestic violence as foreplay just so they can keep pretending to be vanilla. Vanillas are boring, less intelligent, closer to breeders, and not really part of queer culture. They think cunnilingus is the be-all and end-all of lesbian sex. They're lightweights and wimps. They're afraid to go to the edge. They're bland. They look at me like I'm dirt.

My advice to those who engage in this type of name-calling: Stop it. Play safe, love hard, and quit whispering behind each other's backs.

-----------------------------✍-----------------------------
True Testimonial:
One Lesbian Thinks Vanilla and S/M Dykes Have More in Common Than They Think...

"My 'strictly vanilla' friend Christine and I went to a huge warehouse play party in Portland, Maine. Christine is the most vanilla person I've ever met. The whole idea of any kind of power or pain play just doesn't appeal to her at all, but she went

to the party for me, because I had always been 'S/M curious' and a friend of ours had just come out as a major bondage bottom and had invited us to this party so we could check it out. We walked around like little anthropologists, observing a bit of electroshock torture here, a little flogging over there, and as we did this Christine was constantly yawning and complaining that she was bored and that her shoulders ached.

We stumbled across a group of people gathered around a Ping-Pong table who were running a sort of workshop on the art of aesthetic piercing with hypodermic syringe needles. 'OK, who's next?' said the instructor, a guy with a fuzzy, gray poof of hair and a colostomy bag hanging off his gut. The entire crowd of players took a giant step back, leaving my friend Christine in the foreground. 'How about you?' he said to her. 'Care to try it?'

'Um, OK.' Christine whipped off her T-shirt.

The next thing I knew she was facedown over the Ping-Pong table, and when she stood up again there were two rows of eight, for a total of 16, hypodermics fanning out across her upper back. To top it off, the guy had interwoven skeins of colorful threads from needle to needle, creating a whimsical rainbow butterfly pattern. 'Wanna walk around some more?' she asked, as if it weren't 2 A.M. on a Saturday night in a large, dark, perversity-packed warehouse but rather 2 P.M. on a Sunday afternoon in an educational but slightly boring fish aquarium. That's when I realized, just because you're vanilla doesn't mean you can't take pain, and it doesn't mean you're not tough or cool either." —Jean L.

For Vanilla Lesbians: How to Make S/M Friends

- Send a plate of muffins or dark chocolate truffles to your S/M neighbors (S/M dykes love sugar, especially dark chocolate, almost as much as they love dungeons).

- Acknowledge your own inner kinkster. (Do you enjoy being blindfolded, held down, bossed around, or

for your partner to be a little forceful? Do you enjoy blind-
folding your partner, holding her down, bossing her around,
or being a little forceful?)

• Take your favorite sentence about S/M: "I think S/M is ['gross'
or 'wrong' or 'politically incorrect']," and substitute the
phrases 'a fun hobby' or 'a way of life' or 'a calling.'

• Remember that friendships with different types of people are
good.

• Ask yourself daily: Does associating with an S/M dyke (or
other sexual outlaw) trigger my sense of self-directed homo-
phobia?

For S/M Dykes: How to Make Vanilla Friends

• Learn humility. You may not be as edgy as you
think.

• Sadists should let their guard down and relax
every once in a while. It's good for the arteries.

• Have a vanilla lesbian for dinner every month.

• Sponsor a poor vanilla lesbian family.

• Just because one vanilla dyke insults you, it doesn't mean
they're all bad.

Monogamy Schmonogamy

The monogamous and nonmonogamous, while seemingly ill-suited, are in almost constant sexual contact with each other (see chapter titled "Relationship Drama" for more on this dynamic). Some women say they're naturally nonmonogamous. This claim, however, can be used to mask both an intimacy phobia and sexual addiction. Actions speak louder than words:

Naturally Nonmonogamous or Intimacyphobe?

Naturally nonmonogamous: *wants the freedom to sleep with other people*
Intimacyphobe: *exercises that freedom on your anniversary*

Naturally nonmonogamous: *believes it's possible to love more than one person at a time*
Intimacyphobe: *loving more than one person at a time keeps her too busy to meet your family, be home for dinner, or remember your name*

Naturally nonmonogamous: *doesn't want to imitate hetero-patriarchal modes of relating*
Intimacyphobe: *doesn't want to imitate hetero-patriarchal modes of relating— unless it relates to her own sense of panic when you decide to see someone else*

Naturally nonmonogamous: *believes jealousy's bad and should be conquered*
Intimacyphobe: *finds loopholes such as the "anybody but her" loophole, wherein your choice of partner is the problem, not the fact that you slept with someone else*

Naturally nonmonogamous and intimacyphobe: *wishes she could find someone as emotionally secure and evolved as she is*

Naturally Nonmonogamous or Sex Addict?

Naturally nonmonogamous: *wants the freedom to sleep with other people*
Sex addict: *quits her job to have more time to sleep with other people*

Naturally nonmonogamous: *believes it's possible to love more than one person at a time*

Sex addict: *believes it's possible to love more than one person at a time...including several characters in the same porn video*

Naturally nonmonogamous: *doesn't want to imitate hetero-patriarchal modes of relating*

Sex addict: *keeps a row of notches on her belt*

Naturally nonmonogamous: *believes jealousy's bad and should be conquered*

Sex addict: *believes jealousy's bad and should be conquered—unless she's jealous because someone else is getting laid more often than she is.*

True Testimonial:
One Lesbian's Experience in a Poly Relationship

"I was involved as the nonprimary play partner in a poly relationship in which I was friends with all involved. Yes, it was lots and lots of fun. But when you're making the room shake with one lady then having coffee with her life partner the next morning, it gets a little creepy. And it did get weird—I became the confidante of one and the lover of the other. After all the room shakin' was done, any semblance of a friendship was gone." —Arden

----

Pillow Princesses

The term *Pillow Princess* combines the English words *pillow,* which connotes, well, pillow, as in "her head never left the..." and *princess,* which connotes a sort of royal privilege. In short, the

Dyke Drama

Pillow Princess chooses the privilege of never having to reciprocate sexually. There are many different variants of the Pillow Princess, such as the "Pillow Princess and the Pea," who's too delicate to reciprocate, the "White Anglo-Saxon Pillow Princess," who's too stiff to reciprocate, and the "Pillow Princess Leah"— often a social worker—whose daily heroics render her too spent to reciprocate. Many also fall into the category of the "Sleeping Beauty Pillow Princess," who, in the hazy repose of her afterglow, lapses into a deep, deep sleep, making you feel like a bitchy queen. Not many people know this, but a butch or boi bottom has, in some circles, been called a "Pillow Prince."

There are many things we know about Pillow Princesses, yet their existence raises a handful of heretofore unanswered philosophical and moral questions: Is the gay male version called a "Pillow Queen"? And if Pillow Princesses existed in the heterosexual arena, what percentage of heterosexual males would notice?

Life can feel a bit unfair if you're not actually a Pillow Princess but have gained that reputation by way of some false and unfair bad-mouthing. One way to derail the stigma is to get rid of all your pillows. That's right, all of them, from the throws on your sofa to the expensive goose-downs you got for a steal during Stroud's Labor Day sale. If your dog or cat has a little lambswool cushion he or she likes to sleep on, toss that out too. "How can I be a Pillow Princess when I don't have any pillows?" is usually enough to convince a potential lover that what she heard was just idle gossip. After that, it's up to you to put your honey where your mouth is...or whatever.

Interview With a Pillow Princess

Marnie has always defined herself as a "perennial Pillow Princess." I rang her up at her government job in Ann Arbor, Michigan, where she kindly agreed to an impromptu interview.

Where do you live?

With my mother right now, in Ann Arbor.

Do you still consider yourself a perennial Pillow Princess?

And damn proud of it.

Has this ever been an advantage in securing dates?

Oh, yes, hundreds of times. I've been pointed out to people at parties and by bartenders at our local lesbian pickup joint, the Aut Bar. You know those types of women who don't like to be touched? They love me. I get laid all the time! [*laughs*]

Why do you think you became a Pillow Princess?

Well, for me, it's basically just how I'm wired. I have to have at least three [orgasms] and if I don't have three, I'm pissed. I'm disappointed, you know? Disappointed in myself, God, and whomever I'm with at the time. Three or above and I'm cool— but my preference is six. Less than three, forget it. I guess this makes me selfish, but by the time I've actually had six [mind-blowing orgasms], well, I just don't feel like moving afterward. Nope. Not at all. And I know that sounds selfish, but there are ways to rig it so the other woman doesn't mind.

What are those? I mean, how do you keep a woman with her own needs from feeling neglected?

Simple. You use psychology. For example, it's really true that flattery will get you everywhere. Make her feel like she just rocked your world. I usually say something like, "Oh, my God, you stud." I also like to feign catatonia and murmur: "Look what you've done to me." My favorite is to make her get up and write down whatever it was she just did to me so she never ever forgets it. While she's doing that, I take the opportunity to drift off to sleep, or just leave.

Dyke Drama

Sounds a little underhanded...

I'm a Pillow Princess. I'm good at what I do, but it's just what I do. I don't question things.

Think you could pass on some tips for would-be selfish types like yourself?

Why, I'd be proud to—especially if I get paid...

Tips from a Self-Avowed Pillow Princess

• You come first. Literally. Be selfish. Go into the evening/morning/midday/whenever knowing this. Do not be ashamed. Stay away from anyone you might actually get all mushy about. Remember: This is all about the "o" factor, honey. You're on a mission. Stay focused. Have no mercy. Men do this all the time, so sack up and get out there.

• Target-wise, drag is good. We're not talking about the svelte, model-perfect androgynous type lingering in the well-lit corner. No, sir, that one's trouble (unless you're feeling extremely lucky, in which case, you go, sister). I'm talking about the woman in the somewhat ill-fitting suit wearing a nice tie. The nice tie (learn your fabrics: Armani, Burberry, etc.) is a clue that she has the ability to pay for dinner and a hotel room and that she has a little style (you may also kink out later and have her tie you up with it...your choice). Though her woman's body doesn't quite jibe with the cut of a three-button Ralph Lauren (to be expected, generally), the whole drag thing, well, you know, means she needs what you've got. Probably.

• Think of your box as if it's Fort Knox, like it's a turquoise deal from Tiffany tied with a white silky bow. I don't care if you're wearing thrift store togs and are tubby as plain vanilla pudding, walk like your pubes are made of mink. Confidence will open doors, especially to the bedroom.

- Hand in hand with "cunt confidence" is good hygiene. Aside from the standard medical maintenance, maintain a good path in the forest. Shaving's OK but may leave you dry-humping the Xerox machine to relieve the second-day itch. I've found that a pair of small beauty scissors works best. Next, use a good perfume, but not a lot of it. If you can't afford anything better than Windsong, head to a department store counter and get some samples. One good spritz of Christian Dior on a sample card is plenty to rub on the hair downstairs...and only the hair.

- When time is limited, use a nice lube to kick-start things. And think of Angelina Jolie.

- Consider older women. They're generally more experienced and are good cooks. Also, they're not Paris Hilton, so they're more likely to enjoy spoiling rather than being spoiled. In short, they're less demanding of reciprocation and may engage in great conversation after shaking down your tree.

- Stay complimentary before, during, and after your partner's, uh, "performance." By compliments, I mean sounds—really, really loud sounds—as much as actual sentences. Feel free to give directions, but always try to sound porn-movie happy when you do it.

- Be gracious, but be gone. Leave a note, a flower, a personalized thank-you note if you like, but don't stick around. Run out for a pack of smokes and don't return. Also helpful: Keep spare underwear in your glove box. It can save you valuable escape time.

The Pillow Princess-Turned-Butch Top

For those of us who expect reciprocation, no matter how much we love our Pillow Princesses, we may never feel loved back. Probably the worst, most frustrating Pillow Princess I was ever involved with was a pale, ponytail-sporting girl named Meredith, a self-described "intellectual" and "literary type." She was studying to become a literature professor, and her claim to fame was her inability to actually pronounce the word *literature,* which she always called *lidda-cher.* This was not a joke to her but some sort of chronic—and probably genetic—brain fart. Meredith was a classic Sleeping Beauty Princess; she conked out after every orgasm, and it wasn't just with me. In later years I spoke with one or two other women she had slept with, and they always told the same story. Not only was she no good after she came, she wasn't that hot before either. Yet she always complained about never having a girlfriend, or just about women in general. Women were shallow, she could never have the one she wanted, and so on... She despised butches as giving lesbians "a bad name." She preferred to chase after what she called "high femmes."

Years later, in graduate school, Meredith experienced an awakening of her "true identity" and called to tell me about it. She'd decided to claim the part of herself she'd been suppressing all these years: the identity of the butch top.

Two months later, Meredith came for a visit. She'd cut off her ponytail and was wearing a man's tweed suit from a thrift store. It made her look like Pee Wee Herman with a flattop. She told me her queer studies classes at Granola University made her finally feel comfortable with her butch identity. Besides, she was tired of losing all the good femmes to all those swaggering "superbutches." She was giving up her femme-to-femme philosophy, and damn it felt good.

The trouble was, as anyone might guess, butch or femme,

Meredith was missing the point, which was that she was probably the most selfish lover in all of lesbian history, and that wasn't going to change. Her erotic tastes were very bizarre, and possibly bogus. She wanted her earlobes pulled, hard. I was willing to do it despite the fact that it wasn't much fun for me. She wanted it done for hours on end and would just lie there with her eyes closed, smiling this weird smile and licking her lips like a dog. Every once in a while she'd sort of curse. But it wasn't really a curse; it was more like, "Man!" or "Oh, man!" And, you know, if this was foreplay, I wanted it to be shorter. I also don't remember that it made her the slightest bit wet, so I started to think it was just something that felt good—like a massage—and she was only pretending to make it sexual to keep me interested. Instead I felt like an overworked farmhand, milking a cow that had long since gone dry. And it never seemed to take us anywhere. Whether this is above and beyond what your standard Pillow Princess will put you through, I have no idea, but in order to call it sex, there ought to be at least one person who gets to have an orgasm, shouldn't there?

As far as I know, she never did learn how to pronounce *literature.*

The Traumatized Princess

If your lover is a traumatized princess, avoid turning your frustrations into a full-blown dyke drama. Accept that she may never fully enjoy things in the same way you do. Imagine confronting one of your own worst fears (for me, a nightmare that I'm French-kissing Dr. Laura Schlessinger). Think *you* could be nagged into conquering that? At the same time, one is not one's lover's therapist and should be careful about stepping into that role. It's perfectly normal to feel frustrated—even furious—at a lover who balks at doing the one thing you find most pleasurable. Vent to a neutral outside party, someone with a sympathetic ear. (The world is crawling with these people, many of whom will work on a sliding scale.)

Exclusive Top Seeks Pillow Princess

Rigid adherence to "top" and "bottom" roles seems much more acceptable in the gay male community. At the very least, we don't see as many ads with "exclusive top seeks Pillow Princess" in the women-seeking-women section of the personals. Lesbians either expect themselves (perhaps unrealistically) to be more flexible or, like many women, they're interested in becoming well-rounded. (Is this an unconscious desire to please, since society expects us to be malleable?) Many women who took my dyke-drama survey revealed problems with being labeled "top," "bottom," "stone," or "vanilla." Others suffered more under the expectation of role versatility. For example, novelist Rachel W. met a woman via the Internet, leading to a dramatic one-night stand in a hotel room in a city halfway between where each woman lived. Rachel explains:

> She worked in the television industry as a director of a local news show. It started when she wrote me a fan letter and I answered it. (I usually answer all my fan mail but have since sworn off sleeping with any of my readers. It always leads to absolutely disastrous results, and then they know where I live.) Answering her letter led to a whole flurry of e-mail/lust stuff that went on for about a month online.
>
> In her relationships, she was almost always a top, and I am always without fail a bottom, but we decided we wanted to switch. We finally agreed to

meet and have sex and try out our new roles.

In the bar of the hotel we had some martinis, and she went directly into top mode and never left it, which greatly disappointed me because I'd traveled a long way to try to top her and had spent a fortune on my hotel room and my underwear. And she wasn't even a particularly inspired or interesting top. The sex was so-so. Nothing special.

But what *was* special was the fact that she was really nuts. She started a fire in my hotel room during dinner (accidentally setting her napkin on fire by being too drunk and smoking, even though I was in a nonsmoking room and had asked her not to smoke). In the middle of the very expensive room service dinner (the entire tab of which she stuck me for) she left my room to make a "quick trip" to her own room and then she promptly got lost. She couldn't remember her room number. My room was in the upper part of the hotel where you had to have a special elevator key to access the floor, so she couldn't get back to my floor. She was afraid to go down to the lobby to inquire about her own room number or to call me, because she was not completely dressed and it was a busy Friday night in a very nice hotel. She claimed she was riding the elevator half-dressed and in a daze for well over an hour until another guest had a key that accessed my floor. In all that time, she had never managed to remember her own room number, so I had to get dressed and take her there myself.

I couldn't wait to get away from her and was very glad we'd decided to have separate rooms. And still, after the horrible weekend, she wrote me an e-mail asking me to move in with her. No lie.

The above Class IV drama began with the ill-advised act of sleeping with a fan. When it was stirred in with the intent to reverse the top-bottom dynamic, the situation snowballed to encompass three of the five natural disasters of lesbian sex: drunkenness, fire, and absurd formation of emotional attachment (the remaining two being the lopsided three-way and sexually transmitted disease). How many run-of-the-mill dyke-drama components can you identify? (Here are a few for starters: boundary issues, disregard for hotel property, overconsumption of alcohol, cheapskate behavior, etc.)

Dyke Sex Cyberdrama

Our top-meets-bottom story also introduces the topic of sexual contact through the Internet, or cybersex. Lesbians may love to cyber more than any other illicit sex practice. It's possibly the perfect women's transgression: It entails a low risk of physical violence and requires a strong sense of imagination and verbal skill. (Plus it's cheap!) Given all these wonderful advantages, you'd expect to just Google the words "lesbian sex" and pull up tons of Web sites and chat rooms created by and for women. But it's actually the opposite. Yep, that's right: The cybersex arena is just one more woman-space that's been co-opted by men. If only some high-profile activist, a serious lesbian lawyer with N.O.W. or Lambda Legal, could pull out a cell phone and strike a deal with all those knob-kneed and flat-assed old millionaire white dudes who don't want women on their golf courses in Florida: "We'll take care of Martha Burke," she'll say. "We'll give you your stupid old Augusta National Golf Club if you'll get your cronies to give us exclusive control over lesbian cybersex."

Leslie Lange

As it is, there's no real way to tell whether last night's hot cyberlingus session was with a real-live dyke or a balding 55-year-old Mormon male senator. Take Bett W.'s story, for example:

> When I was on tour, I met this Mormon couple. The woman seemed very bi-curious. She was also very hot. We flirted a lot, and when I got back home we started e-mailing. One time we IM'ed for an hour, talking about how she might be able to have a few experiences with women while still being respectful of her husband's feelings. I introduced some nasty talk. We basically had cybersex.
>
> She kept saying, "Wow, this is all so new to me being that I'm Mormon." Well, the next day she sent me an e-mail. She said she had something to tell me and was very embarrassed. It turned out I wasn't e-mailing her at all but her husband. I didn't believe her at first, but then the husband e-mailed me and told me he was very sorry and what he did was wrong. He also said I helped him deal with his feelings of inadequacy regarding his wife's sexuality and my advice helped him a lot. It didn't help enough, however, because three weeks later they decided to get a divorce. The Mormon woman is now in a relationship with another woman.

The preponderance of horny men in cyberland has led to a frenzy of dyke paranoia in which nobody trusts anyone. Roberta G. complained that no matter how many times she attempted cybersex in a lesbian chat room, she found herself repeatedly accused of being a man. "It was very disheartening," she said. "I kind of started to doubt my whole gender identity. I finally just gave up and forgot about it."

Lesbians who cybercheat sometimes learn that their "perfect crime" also leaves a "perfect paper trail." Computer glitches intervene like unforeseen forces hoping to save us from the evils of cybersex addiction. Paula N. explains:

> Gay&Lesbian1 was full. Gay&Lesbian2 booted me out. Ten minutes later, I got on again, and into Gay&Lesbian3. My lover peeked in the room occasionally. I guess seeing me mysteriously hunched over the side of the bed with a tangle of wires leading from phone jacks and all available outlets to my lap troubled her.
> "What are you doing? What's that noise?" she asked.
> "It's the modem, honey. I'm just trying to see if it works."
> "Oh."
> Right in the middle of: "Did I tell you to spread your legs?" the damn keyboard froze. Miraculously, the machine kept receiving IMs, but I couldn't do a damn thing about it. "WHERE ARE YOU? I'M WAITING!!!" she wrote. And it went on and on while I frantically pounded the keyboard.

Many act surprised when they find out their partners consider this "harmless hobby" an actual form of infidelity. The old "I didn't realize this counts as cheating" act works only once, though. Creative excuse-making goes a long way toward preserving a happy marriage.

One nice thing about cybersex: It can be just as hot and just as addictive as regular sex, but there's no need to process afterward, unless you are, of course, a computer processor—in which case there really is no benefit. Currently, there are no statistics available on the frequency of lesbian bed death in the cyberrealm. If you're experiencing a lull in your sex life, cybersex may be a great way to avoid greater intimacy.

My advice about cybersex: If you must have it, be honest with your partner. Bring her in on the secret—even use it as foreplay. If she benefits from your cyberhabit, she's much less likely to resent it. Tell her you want to be her personal porn star and that porn stars use fluffers all the time. (A fluffer is the person who gets the porn star heated up so she or he can perform. Not bad work if you can find it.)

If you don't have a partner, too much cybersex will keep you from getting out of the house. It can also keep you from sleeping, paying your bills, and eating. Poor posture is usually not a turn-on for others. Do not attempt to form a relationship in the real world with your cyberlover. I'm not saying it *can't* happen. I'm just saying it's the least efficient way to get good results, especially when the cyberpool is saturated with straight men, married women, and terminal slouch potatoes like yourself.

Sex Addiction

New York TV producer Tina H. told me that before she went through a 12-step program (and became even more annoying) an evening was never complete without a combination of sex, gin, and cocaine. "I'd go out, drink, do some coke, and see how many women I could have sex with in one night. I think the highest number I ever got to was 26."

Wondering about the logistics of this, as well as the veracity, I asked her, "Wow! How'd you manage that?"

"Well, I'd have a quickie in the bathroom, a ménage à trois at one couple's home, leave, drive back to the bar, pick up another girl and have sex in her car—that's four. She drives home and I go back to the bar one more time and wind up having another ménage with this other couple...and then..."

I kept count on my fingers as she continued. When she finished, I looked up at her. "That's...26."

"Exactly 26," said Tina. "That was the most I ever got in one night. Oh, but there were countless times that I had 23 or 24."

Obviously this could only happen in New York City, where the community is large enough to maintain one's anonymity. In smaller communities the sex addict must generally rely on a reduced number of resources. Having one steady romantic partner and a handful of impromptu "booty calls" gets tricky when any of those booty calls decides to get difficult and start asking tough questions like "If you really love so-and-so, then why do you come to me?" or "How about we go on Jerry Springer?" If you're openly nonmonogamous, your booty call may think it's OK to phone you at home. This is almost always annoying to one's partner.

Can you be a sex addict with only one sex partner? Yes—if you need it so often you're unable to sustain yourself with proper nutrition, or you become dehydrated, or are unable to perform as a productive member of society. (**Note:** A temporary sex addiction often occurs during the early stages of romance.)

You Might Be a Lesbian Sex Addict When...

• You tell your girlfriend: "I think I need some alone time," meaning an entire weekend devoted to your favorite erotica, porn videos, and lesbian cybersex sites.

• At your place of work, you routinely lock yourself in the bathroom during both 15-minute coffee breaks.

Leslie Lange

- Some kind of sexual innuendo is always popping out of your mouth, even at really inappropriate times, such as when you're visiting your grandmother and she asks for help washing her false teeth.

- You've stopped going to your favorite health food store because all the cute clerks there are on to you.

- You're sleeping with men because they're more understanding about sex without strings and, besides, it's easier not to care when they whine about their feelings.

Resources for Sex Addicts: Sex Addicts Anonymous (713) 869-4902; Sex and Love Addicts Anonymous (617) 332-1845; Sexaholics Anonymous (615) 331-6230.

Whether they're sex addicts or not, the notion of sexual freedom or enjoyable sluttiness is a rite of passage for many young or just-out lesbians. We can be just as shallow and irresponsible as our gay male friends, right? We even have our own sex clubs. I'm waiting to see the day when lesbians are getting it on through those crazy glory holes in public restrooms. A glory hole is a small hole between two bathroom stalls created by blow torch, jigsaw, or act of God so that sexual contact can occur without having to smell the other person's breath or body odor. Doesn't that sound fantastic? It's like a giant metal vagina or something.

Lesbian Sex Clubs: Proof or Spoof?

I'm not sure if the whole lesbian sex club thing was ever able to take off, but I doubt it. I've heard lesbian sex clubs have been around since the 1980s, but my only experience with one happened back in the '90s in San Francisco and it was like pulling teeth to get those edgy S.F. dykes to actually do each other in public. At the time, I was seeing this push me-pull you bisexual woman who thought it would be "fun to check out." What I remember is a stuffy warehouse packed with punks. This woman named Mimi, dressed in a studded leather corset, was on stage cracking a bullwhip, shouting, "We are here to FUCK! We are here to FUCK!" and her voice was like, well, it made fucking the last thing I wanted to do. But that was OK, because no one else seemed to want to fuck either. Instead everyone just stood around looking terrified—morbidly afraid to make eye contact. The remainder of the evening was a throwback to the seventh grade, when I wore high-waters to the school dance and tried to show some rhythm but knew it was a lost cause because my older sister had already informed me that I had the worst rhythm of anyone she'd ever seen.

I've heard lesbian sex clubs of the 21st century have had more success when they facilitate "erotic dating games." Who knew a simple round of spin the bottle could do so much for the sexual evolution of our kind? To this day I suspect that it was my awkward energy (and mine alone) that jammed a wrench in the cog of sexual energy at the sex club that night and that, once I left, the entire population of the warehouse heaved a huge sigh of relief and the orgy ensued.

Tips for Would-Be Sex Club Attendees:
• Don't be a fattist, racist, or ageist.
• This is not the place to find "Ms. Right."
• If you like public displays of affection, this is your heaven.
• Play safe—use protection.

Dangerous Lesbians

Certain lesbians are like natural disasters...in bed. She's a klutz, basically, but it's hard not to wonder if she has sublimated feelings of rage, hatred, or disgust. For example, the woman who tries to injure you every time she comes—by head squeezing, neck crunching, or ripping out chunks of your hair—may feel guilty about feeling rapt with pleasure, or she may be selling your curly chestnut locks to wigmakers on eBay. Like the ancient Chinese philosopher who once cut off his own sleeve to avoid waking his beloved kitty, as a matter of chivalry and pride a real dyke must often sacrifice comfort to give her lady the most massive and prolonged "o" possible. *On Our Backs* editor Diana Cage describes her own near-death sex experience in *Box Lunch: The Layperson's Guide to Cunnilingus:*

> From time to time, especially when she was nearing a really big orgasm, her pinky fingers would dig into the sides of my neck, cutting off the blood supply to my brain.... Several times she made me see stars...she was just having a really good time, totally unaware that I was about to enter the light like Carol Ann...

Cage eventually learned to tilt her head in a certain angle so that her carotid arteries were inaccessible to her partner. Her advice for avoiding other injuries? Anticipate the problem and restrict the movement of whatever body part becomes an unwitting weapon. Hold her hands down at her sides or secure her crushing thighs with straps—whatever it takes.

Burning Up For Your Love

A fondness for scented candles puts many lesbians at risk for the conflagrant orgasm. If she insists on doing it with candles nearby yet seems to always kick one over and ignite the blanket or furniture, have her seek professional help immediately before she immolates you both. Remember: Candles should be burned no closer than ten feet from the sex at hand.

Freeway to a Three-way

The three-way, a.k.a. ménage à trois—or just "ménage" (as in "Stacy and I got drunk last night and wound up having a *ménage* with our UPS woman.")—is the sexual adventurer's bungee jump. It's daring but requires no real skill.

Lesbians who've had three-ways just love to let you know about it. "Ever had a three-way?" If a lesbian asks you this (especially when the question is accompanied by an unsubtle facial tic), you can be sure she has either had one and is dying to talk about it, or she has never had one but is hoping you'll be able to help her out with it. In an arena where being known as a wild lover matters, the three-way itself may be rewarding in its ability to improve one's sexual currency. It's also an artificial boost of confidence. If I've been in a ménage (or, as they say in Oklahoma, if I've "done a ménage") and you haven't, I'm more accomplished than you are. The false implication is that I'm also a better lover.

Lesbians, gay men, and straight people all have three-ways. Who knows how frequently? It all seems to be about equal. However, lesbians like to extend all sexual activity into a relationship—and to keep those relationships going as long as possible, no matter how absurd. This is the dyke-drama part of three-ways, a.k.a. the lesbian love triangle.

"When I was in a low-key three-way [relationship] with two other women, I developed a crush on another woman," says novelist Jewelle Gomez. "I introduced my crush to my two lovers and had them put her on the softball team they were coaching. It made for some testy and strange games and even stranger nights at the bar after the games. I felt like I'd created a monster."

You Know Your Love Triangle Is in Trouble When...

- You're greeted with a kiss and smell Eau de Lover #3 on her face—and it does not make you smile.
- All three of you want to wear the same leather jacket out to the club that night.
- You realize three makes for triple the amount of processing (as well as Triple PMS).
- There isn't a tampon to be found in the entire house.
- You're always getting stuck doing the dishes.
- You've struck out on getting to be in the middle for the last three consecutive nights.

Dyke Drama

The One-Time Ménage à Trois

Often a single-event ménage will come about when a drug such as alcohol or opium is involved. But when the drug wears off and you sober up, the whole adventure can feel ridiculous. Someone flips a switch and the light bears down ferociously with interrogative menace. You feel...naked. You are...naked. An onion-shaped mole is exposed under the glare. Yours? Someone else's? No matter. Things will never be the same between the three of you.

Never underestimate the power of sex.

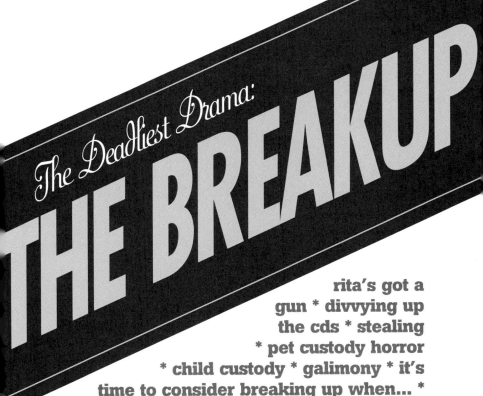

The Deadliest Drama:

THE BREAKUP

rita's got a gun * divvying up the cds * stealing * pet custody horror * child custody * galimony * it's time to consider breaking up when... * how to break up with the least amount of drama * how to sabotage a lesbian wedding * exes who stalk * the never-ending breakup * prolonged post-breakup cohabitation * breakup counseling

.

"...I suspect that some members of the public below her open living room window were probably able to hear me as I wailed and screamed and demanded to know 'WHY, WHY ARE YOU DOING THIS? AND ANYWAY I DON'T LOVE YOU ANYMORE AND I DON'T EVEN KNOW IF I LIKE YOU!!' What they couldn't see was her, just sitting there on the couch looking at me like, 'Don't you get it? It's over.'" —Barbara Raab, "Breakup Breakdowns," NY Blade, 2000*

Rita's Got a Gun

In 1981, *Rubyfruit Jungle* author and horse enthusiast Rita Mae Brown used a handgun to blow out the rear window of Martina Navratilova's retreating BMW in possibly one of the most exciting breakups in dyke-drama history. According to Brown's autobiography *Rita Will,* Martina had left

the gun on the bathroom sink. Rita Mae picked up the gun and told her to get rid of it, presumably because, like many Southern women, Rita Mae doesn't approve of bathroom sink clutter. "She hit

me," writes Brown. "I hit back." This seems an oversimplified way of saying *We engaged in a good old-fashioned fistfight.* No mention was made as to whether Martina's cute little circular John Denver glasses were broken in the scuffle, but at some point—perhaps when Martina's muscular arms got tired, or when she realized Rita Mae still held the pistol—Martina ran off and jumped into the BMW, exhibiting, I'm sure, the same powerful athleticism she used to charge the net at Wimbledon.

Because she had the gun, and was Southern, Rita Mae was

able to aim it, so she blew out the back window. Sixteen years later, in her autobiography, Rita Mae had the following insight to offer about the incident: "...angry and heartbroken as I was, if I'd wanted to hit her she'd be six feet under."

True, if she'd wanted to hit Martina, she could've shot her at point-blank range *before* she got in the BMW. However, when a gun is fired to blow out someone's car window, the trajectory of the bullet does occasionally find the skull of the driver—even if by accident. But, hey, Rita Mae hadn't really wanted to hit Martina—she just, well, wanted to "scare the shit out of her." Everyone knows tennis pros are terrified of loud noises.And a gun makes a pretty loud KABOOM!

"What I did," explained Brown, "was relieve her of moral responsibility for her actions and give her a story she could embellish over the years."

Sigh. If only *all* jilted lesbians could be so magnanimous...and to think Martina didn't even send a thank-you card.

Thankfully, not all lesbian breakups involve the use of firearms. Sometimes it's even worse. I'm talking about the shit that goes down when two dykes are divvying up CDs, for example. Now, that's ugly.

Divvying up the CDs

If I can offer any advice to lesbians who wish to cohabitate, it's to save receipts for all your CDs and save the wrapping paper for any CDs you were given as a gift. You can write the title of the CD on the inside of the wrapping paper and file it away for future use. Another piece of advice: In the weeks before an impending breakup, keep a watchful eye on your tunes. They're known to disappear long before cohabitation is officially called off, and once that happens you can kiss those suckers goodbye. I cannot for the life of me figure out how something that costs

$15 can have such an enormous impact on a person's emotional well-being, but it can, and it does. The value of the CD neither lesbian has listened to in over five years? Priceless.

There's also the case of the anonymous CD, the CD that's missing that no one can name:

"Where's my CD?"

"What CD?"

"You know, the one with that singer, the one we liked so much at Lilith Fair that year..."

"I don't know what or who you're talking about."

"Just confess. You've got it and you're using the fact that I can't remember her name against me."

"Well, if you can't remember her name, how important could she have been to you?"

Emergency Intervention:
Co-owned Possesions

Co-owned possessions aren't a bad idea, but breakups have a way of making objects that were seemingly worthless to both parties miraculously skyrocket in monetary and sentimental value. When doing battle over co-owned objects, try to get the ones worth the most dollars and cents. Sentiment fades over the years and many of these items wind up at garage sales or on eBay before a year has passed. If you're sure to battle viciously over a specific object, arrange to have it disappear before the breakup is final.

Stealing

Divvying things up politely is hard work. Stealing is much, much easier, and way more satisfying. In many of my breakups I felt I'd been cheated, that a significant part of my very soul had been taken from me and I could never get it back. It's this line of thought, among others, that inspires exes to steal from each other. If she took your soul, don't you at least deserve something to show for it, something like the framed print of frolicking mermaids you gave her on her last birthday (before she broke up with you)? Or that Patagonia jacket she never wore but that fit you perfectly? Among lesbians surveyed, items reported stolen during a breakup have included: a barbecue, fur-lined wrist restraints, diaries, refrigerator magnets, a mortar and pestle, clothes, commuter mugs, a prosthetic limb, steak knives, a beloved dildo, a badminton set, and a house.

Pet Custody Horror

Disputes over pets are a circus of absurdity, with one partner always claiming to have paid all the vet bills while the other believes she has a greater emotional bond with the animal because she picked up all of its poop. Ultimately, the toughest ex wins, the one who's willing to be a bad guy. When both exes are willing to be bad guys, things really get ugly.

Pat D. was convinced her jealous ex had hired a private investigator to spy on her. She believed this not because she was paranoid, but because a dark blue sedan with tinted windows had been parked in front of her house all night, and when she took a trip to the grocery store it pulled out away from the curb and followed her down the street. Enraged at this invasion of her privacy, Pat pulled over, got out of her car, and stomped over to the offending driver of the sedan who'd pulled over just behind her because he had indeed been following her. A tall, imposing sort of dyke, Pat began to shout accusations at the man behind the wheel. As this continued, a petite young woman (actually a teenager) in the car got out on the passenger side, dashed over to Pat's car, and dragged out Pat's utterly bewildered 11-year-old chocolate lab, Pookie (who was, by all accounts, utterly bewildered most of the time anyway). Clutching the 66-pound dog to her chest, its rear legs swinging in pendular fashion, the 98-pound dognapper hobbled back to the sedan. "I was so stunned," said Pat, "that I didn't even have a chance to react before the sons of bitches peeled out."

Q: What kind of woman hires a father-daughter team of dognappers to retrieve a chocolate lab?

A: An Amazon warrior with change in her pocket.

Ashes to Ashes

Due to the high risk of escalating drama, duplicity can be the best way to settle animal-remains custody issues between two lesbians. Rachel S. shared a dog with her ex, and when the dog died the ex demanded the ashes. When Rachel confided to the crematorium owner how sad this made her, how she felt the dog had always been hers, the man decided to split the ashes between the two women. "He promised not to tell my ex she was only getting half her dog."

Pet Custody Rule of Thumb

The welfare of the animal is a priority. Animals owned before the relationship should go to the original owner—except in cases where the owner is crappy. For example: Two women live around the corner from one woman's ex, and out on the street they start seeing a cat the previous couple once shared. "Mewsie Man" is very old, has been surgically declawed, and has never been an outdoor cat. One day he shows up puking on their doorstep and they keep him for a week before the original owner puts up a MISSING CAT sign. The former partner returns Mewsie reluctantly, concerned about the elderly tom's welfare but not wanting to make trouble. The next time Mewsie shows up at the door, they keep him. When the ex calls to say the cat is lost again, they tell her she's a crappy owner and that they'll be keeping Mewsie for good. Though the ex may get angry, the couple is doing the best thing for the cat.

How to Settle a Cat Custody Battle in Which the Cat Belongs to Both Partners

Cats are place-oriented animals. Whoever gets the house gets the cat. If both partners move out, the one who moves into the biggest apartment or house gets the cat, although in the event of a tie, the partner with the most—or *most interesting* (as decided by the cat)—cat toys wins. This rule does not apply in the case of abuse or neglect.

How to Settle a Dog Custody Battle in Which the Dog Belongs to Both Partners

Dogs are people-oriented animals. Whoever took care of the majority of the dog's feeding, walking, and waste collection should get the dog. This rule does not apply in the case of abuse or neglect.

How to Settle an Exotic Pet (Rat, Snake, Gila Monster, Ferret) Custody Battle in Which the Animal Belongs to Both Partners

Go with whoever still wants the gnarly creature.

Leslie Lange

Child Custody

It's crap, pure hypocritical crap, when one biological mother can use antigay laws to keep her ex away from the child they helped raise together. It's also crap when a deadbeat lesbian mom uses antigay laws to squeak out of paying child support.

If you're on the bad end of the stick in either of these situations, you might want to buck up and consider becoming a high-profile poster child for the marriage equality movement. Give speeches and rabble-rouse, tell your story to as many folks as you can, get on TV, volunteer to be interviewed for a documentary, and so on.

Also, I don't know if you can get on *Judge Judy* with one of these cases, but if it's possible, I say do it. Even if the law's not on your side, I believe old J.J. will do what's right.

If you're one of the women using these laws to your advantage, keep an eye on your karma, sister. It's going down the tubes.

Galimony

As if catcalling fans and homophobic comments from the likes of preppy Lindsay Davenport and supersnot Martina Hingis aren't enough, the galimony suit is a rite of passage for lesbian professional tennis players. Marilyn Barnett brought one against Billie Jean King in 1981 (leading Billie Jean to kiss her husband on the lips—see, I do love him!—during a press conference). Former beauty queen Judy Nelson had the balls to sue Martina in that great state of sodomy laws, Texas. Because Nelson videotaped their financial agreement, she scored about $2 million in an out-of-court settlement. (Amélie, I hope you're reading this right now.)

In a perfect world, we wouldn't have galimony, of course. We'd have alimony just like anybody else—and it wouldn't be a big deal.

How to Prevent an Ugly Galimony Suit
- Stay broke at all costs.
- Stay single at all costs.
- If you cannot stay broke and single, and you're a high-profile individual in any field, find someone who makes more money than you do.
- Don't make any promises you don't intend to keep, especially on videotape.
- Do not become a professional women's tennis player.

The ultimate sensational lesbian galimony story:

Love Match: Nelson vs. Navratilova, by Sandra Faulkner, with Judy Nelson (Carol Publishing, 1993)

It's Time to Consider Breaking Up When…
You dream of strangling her, and it's not a nightmare.

You're a Little Late With Your Breakup When…
You dream of strangling her, and it's not even a dream.

How to Break Up With the Least Amount of Drama…
- Slink off quietly.
- Repress everything you feel for five years.
- Watch comedy movies till you finally cheer up.

Leslie Lange

How to Break Up With the Most Amount of Drama

- Think only of yourself.
- Consume high–alcohol–content liquor and trash your ex all over town.
- Seek revenge. (In cases where you've been dumped for another woman, hold in your anger till the time is ripe, such as the day of their wedding.)

How to Sabotage a Lesbian Wedding

- Phone every wedding shop in town and rent all tuxedos and cummerbunds. Also, make sure local party shops are conveniently out of rainbow streamers and balloons.

- Call prospective guests and tell them the couple's wedding invitations are not made out of recycled paper.

- Print out all your ex's old love letters and deliver them to the new woman's home. If these are in e-mail form, change the dates so that they look recent.

- If you live in a small town, bribe the head/owner of the local Lion's Club, bowling alley, banquet hall, Rotary Club, veteran's facility, etc., to double-book the evening.

Dyke Drama

If none of the above brings their plans to a halt, don't worry. You can still ruin the wedding reception:

- Secretly spike the baba ghanoush at the reception with chicken broth, then make a crazy scene: "Oh, my god! You said this was a vegan buffet!" Throngs of dykes will flee.

- Go to a truck stop a half hour before the reception and invite a bunch of smelly truckers to enjoy the festivities.

- Photocopy all the compromising photos you have of your ex and covertly place them on each centerpiece.

- Dirty-dance with your ex's new girlfriend's ex—topless.

Note: While slashing tires, verbal harassment, and kidnapping may sound appealing in the heat of the moment, remember, these are all illegal and may be punishable by fines and jail time (check your local and state laws). As always, the author strongly discourages revenge-seeking activities of any kind.

Exes Who Stalk

Soon after her breakup, author Ellen Orleans learned what it was like to be stalked by an ex. "She made me want to become a Luddite. She was clearly a technology abuser, leaving long, anguished messages on my home answering machine asking that we get back together. These would be immediately followed by short, angry messages on my business voice mail saying she never wanted to talk to me again. Shortly after, I'd receive rambling, incoherent, and highly ungrammatical e-mails, starting the whole process all over again."

Adelina C.'s crazy ex followed her at night to see if Adelina was going out to clubs. She stole pages from Adelina's diary and sent them to her in the mail. Any lines that said something remotely nice about her were highlighted. "Right," commented Adelina, "like this was supposed to remind me how I felt about her?!"

Sometimes a bitter ex will make outrageous accusations or requests to keep you obliged to her. Jewelle Gomez's first ex demanded money to reimburse her for food Jewelle had eaten when she'd lived with her. "She actually totaled up how many meals I'd had in the nine months we lived together, including glasses of wine."

When an ex stalks or harasses, she will often flip-flop between trying to make up with you and trying to hurt you as much as you're hurting her. In these cases, the best strategy is to have as little to do with her as possible—just like with any ordinary stalker. Tell her you'd like to have no further contact, then back your statement up by never contacting her, even if you need a favor and she's your only friend. It's time to find some new ones. (See chapter titled "Dyke Stalkers" for more information.)

True Testimonial:
One Lesbian's Tale of a Twisted Breakup

"Lori just couldn't accept that I didn't want to see her anymore. She had bouquets of red roses delivered to my office. She sent me a teddy bear. She kept call-

ing me at work and at home. She wanted to 'just be friends.' I didn't. She e-mailed me constantly. Finally she seemed to let up. And then I found out she was keeping in touch with my daughter, who was 12 at the time, via e-mail, as a way to keep connected to me in some weird way. When I called Lori and read her the riot act, warning her to stay away from my kid, she pretty much stopped bothering me, except for the call every few months after that, asking me if I wanted to have lunch. Which I didn't.

The only problem with all this was that I had stored my snow tires in her garage since I was living in an apartment and had no storage space for them. When I stopped seeing her, it was very abrupt. Lori had some sort of psychotic breakdown because my daughter let Lori's dog into the house from the backyard without wiping mud off its paws. She was fanatically clean. She started yelling about how her property (her living room rug) was being destroyed and just generally lost it. At that moment I said I was leaving and I grabbed my daughter and we fled from the house. Meanwhile Lori was yelling at me to never come back if I left. At that point I couldn't get my tires out of the garage—I was basically running for my life. I was quite scared. Later I didn't want to deal with having to go get the tires, since I'd have to see her. After some months passed, one morning around 3 A.M. I drove out to her house, which was pretty far away. I quietly opened the back gate, went into the garage, loaded my snow tires into my car, and sped away." —Melissande

---

The Never-Ending Breakup

Never-ending breakups are not really breakups—they're relationships. Lesbians who aren't familiar with the concept of having normal ups and downs in relationships become exultantly happy during the ups then tell all their friends they're breaking up during the downs. This is common with the drama couple (see page 137), with younger lesbians, or with any lesbian who may need to feel like something meaningful and intense is going on in her life, even if she has to invent it.

Leslie Lange

The never-ending breakup is always cut short by what's known as "separation anxiety." Once this sets in, the couple rushes back into each other's arms until the next down phase. Sometimes this cycle happens over a very short span of time, as when Jackie tells Marta, "That's it, I'm leaving you. I'm going to sleep on the couch."

"Fine!" says Marta. "Get your things out by tomorrow or I'll toss them out for you!"

Jackie goes out to sleep on the couch. *Oh,* she realizes. *It's lonely out here.*

Meanwhile Marta thinks, *I miss her already.*

Five minutes later: Can you say "makeup sex"?

Prolonged Post-Breakup Cohabitation

The world's record for longest post-breakup cohabitation (PPBC) has to go to my lesbian great-aunt Kristy, who lived in a small motor home in Nocona, Texas (once known for its boot factory, which has since "closed for good"), with her ex, Tamika, for 47 years until she died. Kristy suffered from two major problems: She lived in a community where there were no other lesbians, and she was a born-again Christian with faith-based self-loathing. She had an awfully hard time hooking up with anyone new.

Most lesbian exes don't live together as long as Kristy and Tamika, but let's face it, it is hard for us to leave our precious nests. We're sometimes like cats—place-oriented rather than person-oriented. And proximity to an ex is convenient when one's favorite hobby is tormenting her with really sadistic mind games.

For your own sanity, and the sanity of others, after a breakup do what you can to move out as soon as possible. If you can find a place to stay while you're looking for a new one, do it. Make a list of friends who might put you up—and call them all.

Consider spending a week at a nice hotel. You'll be surprised what a little distance can do for your psyche, and soon you'll be on your way to a healthier, happier life.

Breakup Counseling

Breakup counseling is never called "breakup counseling"; it's called "couples counseling." This can be confusing, especially once you've broken up with someone and you actually need counseling to recover from a breakup. But that's called "individual therapy."

Breakup Meltdown

The best kinds of lesbian breakups occur when two women who deeply respect each other realize they're moving in separate directions and come to a mutual agreement that it's just not working anymore. I have never seen this kind of lesbian breakup, though I have seen lesbians try to pass it off as such...especially when those lesbians are celebrities who've been together 12 years and have two kids by David Crosby.

The worst kinds of breakups are the kind that make you crazy. For example:

• Everything seems to be moving along just fine when...BLAMMO! "I'm sorry, but I'm leaving you. I don't love you anymore and I'm not sure I ever did. Bye." (Translation A: Your girlfriend is a serial monogamist with an internal clock that just went off and told her it was time to move on. Translation B: You're deluded or distracted or dense, and at any rate you haven't been paying attention to reality for a while.)

• She tells you she's leaving you and—by the way—there's someone else.

- She tells you she's leaving you and—by the way—she's really straight.

  Such breakups bring out a special brand of lesbian insanity that may include:

- Tying up a bundle of her old love letters and photos of the two of you and placing them in the garbage disposal.

- Alternating pleading phone messages with angry phone messages.

- Writing pages and pages of woeful, distraught, and angry words in your journal, then burning the whole thing in the makeshift fire pit you constructed in the center of your living room.

- Stalking her new lover.

- Consuming (or authoring) mass quantities of self-help books.

  Long ago, my older and more mature girlfriend decided she needed time to sort out her feelings for me and that a good way would be for me to move out of our apartment for an undetermined period of time while she immersed herself in an affair with a waifish, rat-tailed baker chick. I said, "OK" and went to stay with an ex of mine, who was a social worker for the juvenile prison system and none too thrilled about it (applies to both her job *and* my coming to stay with her).

  Needless to say, rather than putting an end to that drama, I chose to become obsessed with the rat-tailed baker chick and whether she would continue to see my girlfriend if she

knew she was acting as a mere diversion while my lover sort-
ed out her feelings for me. At 3 A.M.—unable to fall asleep—I
got up and drove to the downtown bakery where I knew the
baker would be alone, firing up the ovens for the morning
bread and muffins.

Just outside the bakery I hopped up and down in front of
a narrow six-foot-high window catching glimpses of the
baker while she worked. She looked up at one point and we
locked eyes. I walked around to the front door and she let me
in. I sat on a high stool and sobbed. She brought me a hot-
from-the-oven blueberry muffin and a glass of cold milk. It
was delicious.

Of course, the baker didn't care that she was a diversion.

(Oddly enough, 15 years later I got on a public bus in Eugene,

Oregon, and the baker, now a bus driver, was driving my bus. I sat in the very back and locked eyes with her in the rearview mirror, just like I had through the narrow window that day at the bakery. Neither of us acknowledged the other, but we each knew who the other one was. I couldn't help it—I telepathically communicated: *Not with her now, are you? Nope, now you're my bus driver.*)

Reading List for Breakup Recovery

The Lesbian Love Companion: How to Survive Everything From Heartthrob to Heartbreak, by Marny Hall (HarperSanFrancisco, 1998)

Unbroken Ties: Lesbian Ex-Lovers, by Carol S. Becker (Alyson Books, 1988)

Write From the Heart: Lesbians Healing From Heartache, by Anita L. Pace (Baby Steps Press, 1996)

Suggested Reading
(If the Above Doesn't Help)

Who Moved My Cheese?: An A-Mazing Way to Deal With Change in Your Work and in Your Life by Spencer Johnson, M.D. (Putnam, 1998)

DRUNK DRAMA

what is drunk drama? * barroom drama * veteran detroit lesbian bouncer tells all * drunken lesbian literary types * sloppiness as handled in polite lesbian society * dating an alcoholic * creating an alcoholic * party pda's we love to hate * resources for lesbians who can't hold their liquor and don't seem to care

"It seems that when a girl gets drunk, she thinks she has the right to put her hands on your ass. She doesn't." —Arden

What Is Drunk Drama?

There are two kinds of lesbian drunk drama. The first is any kind of usual drama that features a drunken lesbian (such as a public spectacle or brawl), two tipsy lesbian PMSers, or a pet custody battle that would never have resulted in a trip to the emergency room if it weren't for a little ol' bottle of Stoli. The second is the drama that is made over someone's excessive drinking or being an

alcoholic—whether she actually is or not. Often the two types combine for a third version, which is always classified at the level of Class IV to VI drama.

There are many types of lesbian drinkers, from the dyke who

can't hold her liquor and occasionally does something really stupid to the constant perfume and Binaca abuser who thinks she's fooling the world. Entire books have been written on drinking and drinkers—and lesbian drinking and drinkers—and there are 12-step parties going on all over the place chock-full of lesbians (though mainly they're chock-full of nuts).

This chapter concerns itself with the actual events of drunk dyke drama and how, in these booze-ridden situations, a Super Sappho can surmount the entire ordeal.

Barroom Drama

A lot of drunk dyke drama takes place in bars. Don't ask me why, but drinkers seem to gravitate to these types of places, possibly because of all the alcohol they serve. In order to avoid becoming injured in a barroom brawl, it helps to familiarize yourself with the primary hazards of the environment.

Seven Most Common Barroom Projectiles
1. shot glass
2. liquid contents of a martini glass (upscale version)
3. liquid contents of a pint glass (working-class version)
4. billiard ball
5. the cocktail napkin she wrote her number on (before flirting with someone else)
6. handful of margarita salt
7. shouted beads of saliva, which may carry influenza virus or staphylococcus bacteria

Six Most Common Barroom Weapons
1. pool cue
2. chair
3. broken bottle

4. empty bottle
5. upended cocktail table
6. aluminum softball bat

Seven Primary Instigators of Drunken Dyke Drama

1. the jilted lover
2. the affronted butch or macho lesbian
3. two or more lesbians competing for the attentions of the same woman
4. any softball player or other sports dyke—especially after a loss, and especially if engaged in beer-drinking games with players from another team
5. any dyke talking in a very loud voice
6. someone who has just lost at pool
7. drunk dyke trying to get the bartender to serve her one more drink

When in a lesbian bar, avoiding the primary instigators of dyke drama while keeping an eye out for the top seven projectiles and the top six weapons should ensure a safe and enjoyable evening out. It is also helpful to familiarize yourself with the weapons of choice for each of these brawling types. For example, a dyke talking in a loud voice is more likely to infect you with her saliva than to throw margarita salt in your eyes, while softball dykes are known for hurling billiard balls and taking swings at women with their bats. Butches and other macho dykes will rarely throw, but they will swing pool cues. Of course, it takes practice to be on top of all this while still finding time to converse with your friends, but you'll find it's worth the extra work and practice. When you think of what can happen, there's really no alternative.

------------------------------✍------------------------------

True Testimonial:

Veteran Detroit Lesbian Bouncer Tells All...

"Oh, honey. I used to work as the bouncer in a dyke bar, and I've seen more than my share of drama. Butches going after each another with pool cues. One butch telling another, 'If you're gonna keep looking at me like that, you'd better put on a skirt.' A femme grabbing her partner by the hair and dragging her away from a fight. A femme grabbing her partner by the tit to drag her away from a fight. Girls storming into bathrooms to see whether their girlfriends were really alone in there. Girls storming into bathrooms to see whether their girlfriends were really alone in there and finding them very much not alone. Girls throwing drinks in each other's faces, slapping each other. Cops getting called. Restraining orders out the ass. (I used to get a weekly update from a cop pal about who had a 209A against whom and what the terms were (for example, if it was a 'whoever gets there first gets to stay' kind of deal versus an 'X cannot be within 500 feet of Y under any circumstances kind of deal,' etc.). I've been dragged into court to testify at restraining order hearings. Repeatedly. I've seen girls ripping each other's earrings out. Drunken softball butches spilling secrets of clandestine team hookups in front of all, including the partners of the girls who were doing the hooking up. It was bad news. Want to see a team polarize instantly? I don't think so." —J.D.

------------------------------❧------------------------------

Drunken Lesbian Literary Types

Lots of lesbian literary figures—including Djuna Barnes, Patricia Highsmith, and Ernest Hemingway*—enjoyed being blotto all the time. This has led many literary-leaning lesbians to assume that if they drink a lot, they too will have brilliant

---

*Based on his professed desire to have sex with Gertrude Stein, many believe Hemingway was not a repressed male homosexual, as some claim, but a tormented lesbian-identified male.

Leslie Lange

minds and write beautiful prose that will catapult them to fame. Not so. They are more likely to wind up boorish hecklers at poorly attended book signings, as author Bett Williams describes below:

> I was giving a reading and a heckler in the audience was making it nearly impossible to continue.
> "I'm from Philly," she kept saying.
> "Will you go away if I kiss you?" I said.
> "I'm from Philly," she kept saying, getting all up in my face.
> "Well, then get the fuck back to Philly," said a voice from the back of the bar. The woman turned around and charged toward the voice, which turned out to be that of my girlfriend, Silvia. Someone tried to block them, but the woman reached over to grab her. Silvia slapped her across the face, hard. The woman started pulling her down the stairs, and Silvia flipped her around backward with a sophisticated martial arts move over a railing and held her there by her elbow and her hair. Security came. They weren't there earlier because I guess they didn't expect these sorts of things to happen at a lesbian literary event.

The above situation might well have been avoided if:

(a) this literary event were not held in a bar
(b) security had been present from the beginning
(c) the author's girlfriend had not also been drunk
(d) all of the above

Correct answer: (d) all of the above

Dyke Drama

Sloppiness as Handled in Polite Lesbian Society

I'm sitting at a dining table over a delicious plate of crab cakes with a couple of very nice Manhattanite lesbians who were kind enough to let me sit at their table and—although they don't know it yet—pick up my tab. Morgan and Nancy and I are having some wine with our crab cakes, and I've just turned on my digital recorder. Nancy wants to talk about their friend Blaine, who gets out of hand when she has too much wine. So here we are, having too much wine ourselves, talking about someone else who has too much wine. Isn't it all *too much*?

Nancy: This woman, Blaine, has always been unbelievably attracted to my lover, like *historically.* And I understand that Morgan's a pretty woman, but you know how some people just really have a certain chemistry with just ONE person that they've ever met in their entire life. Well, for this woman, it is Morgan. I mean, I can tell she's just nuts about her—isn't she Morgan? [*Morgan laughs*] And, I mean, Morgan is so sweet and accommodating that when this woman is completely out of control she's just very diplomatic about it and tries to calm her down. Unfortunately, when this woman drinks she is like night and day. She's like a werewolf who comes out with this supersexualized alter ego."

Morgan: And she's normally very shy and quiet.

Nancy: It's true. She'll be perfectly reserved and appropriate, then once she's had a few glasses of wine her face gets red and she unleashes all this really...what is it?...really odd lascivious behavior toward Morgan.

Morgan: I just have to say something. Nancy clearly was with me. The time, I remember, it was New Year's Eve. We had all gone out to dinner. We came back. I think we had, we were doing...

Nancy: We were singing karaoke.

Morgan: Yeah, karaoke, or something.

Leslie Lange: On a home karaoke machine?

Morgan: [*amused*] Yes. And anyway, so I was just sitting there, I mean, I was just sitting on the couch...

Nancy: Innocently enough, really.

Morgan: And Blaine comes up to me, and she starts saying, "You know, I've always loved you..."

Nancy: Which she has said before...

Morgan: [*imitating Blaine*] "I'm just so attracted to you. You know, you're the woman I want..." And her girlfriend's there, by the way.

Nancy: It's so absurd!

Morgan: Her girlfriend is there, but she's off to the side—you know, someone who obviously has no self-esteem and just...and just lets this go on.

Nancy: She just lets it go on.

Morgan: So she says to me, "I've always loved you. I've always wanted you," you know, "blah, blah, blah," and then she comes at me, and she tries to *make out* with me.

Nancy: She really does. She just jumps on her.

Morgan: And, you know, I don't want to push her away in a rude way, so I just say, "It's OK, Blaine. It's all right." That was just the one time, but there was another time...

Leslie Lange: Did she sit on your lap?

Morgan: Well, there was another time. This was even more embarrassing. I had an Academy Awards party. We were all in my den. I had the TV on and there were a lot of people in there. Well, Blaine comes in and sits next to me and she starts again with, "I'm so attracted to you, I really want you..." and she starts trying to kiss me on my neck, I mean, all over my neck, and I'm telling you...people are right there. And they're all trying to act like they don't see it because it's so out of char—I mean, it's so weird for her to do this with me.

Leslie Lange: [*getting kind of turned on*] Wow.

Morgan: She was just coming at me and I didn't want to embarrass her, so I just...

Leslie Lange: Yes, I understand. You're kind...kind to a fault.

Nancy: [*laughing*] Yeah!

Morgan: I just keep telling her, "It's OK, Blaine" and "Don't do this, Blaine" and "I like you as a friend, Blaine."

Leslie Lange: Were you there, Nancy?

Nancy: No, that was another time. But it's just to demonstrate that she keeps repeating this. Oh, and then she walks off—and Morgan has white floors—well, she walks off and spills the red wine all over the white floors.

Leslie Lange: White floors? What kind of white floors?

Morgan: Oh, a white shag carpet.

Nancy: Can you imagine someone spilling red wine all over a white shag carpet? That's not OK.

Leslie Lange: Definitely not.

Morgan: I didn't yell at her. I just cleaned it up later.

Leslie Lange: You're very nice. Maybe too nice, eh? [*nudges Nancy*] What's Blaine's girlfriend like?

Morgan: I think she just excuses it as something Blaine does when she's drunk. But they have a strange relationship anyway. I mean, I've heard they're very verbally abusive toward each other. I think they even have, you know, actual physical fights, and that they're both just very volatile and crazy people. But that's just the kind of tension they thrive on, and it keeps them together.

Leslie Lange: Oh, so Blaine coming over and kissing on you could be their form of foreplay.

Morgan: Yeah, like the beginning of a really good fight when they get home, a fight that ends in some really passionate lovemaking.

Nancy: That certainly isn't *my* kind of foreplay.

Morgan: Yeah, but you aren't really upset... I mean, Nancy sees me giving her the eye, like, *oh, no, here she comes again...*

Nancy: Yeah, I think it's just entertaining to me.

Morgan: It's just...so off the wall.

Nancy: It's off the wall, and it's actually sad.

Leslie Lange: All dyke drama is ultimately sad, isn't it? [*I'm still hoping Morgan and Nancy will pick up the tab.*]

Morgan: Well, she's like stumbling around falling over.

Nancy: It *is* embarrassing.

Leslie Lange: And if this were a man treating you this way, how would you react?

Morgan: Oh, much harsher. I'd just push him away and tell him to get out of my house. But Blaine's a friend; I know her, and I don't want to embarrass her.

Leslie Lange: It's interesting how here we are lesbians and we have all these lesbian friends, and that if a man were to act that way he'd be such a—forgive my language—asshole, but we're so tolerant of each other. Which is in some ways bad, and in some ways kind of nice.

Nancy: And she's not physically threatening like a man would be. She's just a little lady...

Leslie Lange: Oh, yes, little ladies get away with everything. They're like small dogs, like long-haired miniature dachshunds.

Nancy: She's harmless enough. She just can't hold her liquor. [*laughs*]

Dyke Drama

The above situation might be remedied by:

(a) Blaine being served only white wine, never red, and never being allowed on the carpet

(b) Taking the incident more seriously rather than inviting Blaine to come over and embarrass herself repeatedly. Blaine should be confronted about her behavior once she sobers up.

(c) A concerned friend giving Morgan and Nancy a few tips on how to run a party: Plastic floor covering is an essential safeguard against spills.

(d) Morgan giving Blaine a spin. Hell, why not a threesome?

Answer: Should be obvious, but it's (b) and (c).

Dating an Alcoholic

Someone who gets drunk and does something embarrassing is not necessarily an alcoholic. Someone who gets drunk and does something embarrassing *a lot* probably is, and it may look something like what happened to erotic novelist Marilyn Jaye Lewis:

> She was funny, smart, career-oriented, and great in bed. But as soon as she started drinking, she became a monster. She spoke loudly in bars and nice restaurants and said really foul, obscene things. Her foul mouth really attracted negative attention to us, which humiliated me. Once she soaked a paper napkin in her water glass and threw it in my face because she thought it was funny—we were dining with another couple at the time. If we were home alone in bed, she was usually fine. Being in crowds tended to make her feel insecure and that's when she would

come unglued and start drinking and saying insulting things. At one Sunday brunch she drank 32 mimosas in one sitting (granted, it was a large group of women and the brunch went on for several hours, but still). She loudly called me a red devil with horns and said that I had a snake in my ass—among other flattering things. Directly after that, it was over between us

If you're involved with an alcoholic, sober or not (or if this is the only type of woman you like to date), check in with www.codependents.org or www.al-anon.alateen.org.

Creating an Alcoholic

There's a certain type of lesbian (often a "serious lesbian" but not always) who sees an alcoholic in whomever she is near. Perhaps she's the child of alcoholics. Perhaps she's the ex of a particularly nasty and violent alcoholic. Perhaps she's a sober alcoholic herself. Perhaps she's none of the above but just paranoid. Whatever the reason, her feelers are out for possible signs of alcoholism, and they're totally stuck on overdrive. If, for example, you order wine with your meal, she tells you she thinks you may have a problem. If you swallow a gulp of wine with your communion at midnight Mass, she wants to check you into a rehab center. And so on. (Refer all creators to the reality check Web site www.TruthorFiction.com.)

Party PDAs We Love to Hate

I am not against public displays of affection (PDAs) per se. But I do believe there's a classy way and a nonclassy way to behave—and this goes for gay men, heterosexuals, bisexuals, and trannies too. There are three types of PDAs that get worse when lesbians drink, especially at bars, potlucks, barbecues, barbecue-potlucks,

Dinah Shore Weekend (which doesn't count because anything goes at Dinah), and fund-raisers. They are: lap-sitting, proprietary touching, and conversational exhibitionism.

Lap-Sitting

Once I was at a lesbian barbeque that included a group of my girlfriend's coworkers and the women from one coworker's rowing group. (Classic formula for a lesbian barbecue: A group of coworkers meets up with a group of sport fanatics. Firefighter lesbians meet up with local softball league lesbians. Lesbian physicians meet lesbians training for the AIDS Ride, etc....) Anyway, I noticed a very cute Bridget Fonda type glancing with a slightly panicky expression toward a woman sitting three patio chairs away. Her discomfort was evident—knuckles white at the ends of the plastic armrests of her chair, body language like that of a repulsed talk show guest. In this case, the offending party had her wide white cargo-shorted ass planted firmly on Bridget's left thigh.

Bridget had fallen prey to that most feared of all lesbian social offenders: the lap-sitter.

At first I made the wrong assumption that the lap-sitter was an insecure girlfriend, exhibiting that sort of boundless territorialism known as proprietary touching. (And I continued to make this wrong assumption as the lap-sitter whispered something into Bridget's ear with what looked to be hot breath and pulled back to give her a sloppy stare.)

Bridget suffered through all this until finally the lap-sitter staggered up to fetch herself the beer that would launch her consumption level into the double digits. For a second, Bridget's left leg remained where it was, blanched and incapable of movement. She used her hands to slowly straighten her knee and vigorously pumped her foot to renew the sensation and blood supply. No sooner had she accomplished this—her limb's color now matching the other's—than her lap was once again occupied, this time on the right thigh, by a bony-assed brunette with very, very blue eyes (they were tinted contacts). Bridget looked ready to break down and cry.

When Blue Eyes stood to exchange hugs with a couple who'd just entered, Bridget stood slowly and, after an initial step whereupon her knee buckled and she had to grab the chair to steady herself, limped off toward the bathroom. Fascinated by what I'd just witnessed—and possibly attracted to Bridget myself—I sprang from my chair and went after her. I found her in a short bathroom line and introduced myself as the author of a book on dyke drama. When she heard that, she had an atypical reaction, meaning that her eyes didn't gloss over and she didn't look for any escape hatch that I could observe. Instead she gripped my forearm with what I perceived was excitement. It turned out that her knees were beginning to buckle on her again and she was grabbing me for support. Still, I was determined to take advantage of the moment. "My girlfriend has been through more drama," Bridget (whose name turned out to be Barb) told me. "She has the best stories. We'll go find her when I get out of the bathroom."

"I'd rather talk to you," I said, "about all those lesbian lap-sitters. I assume not one was your girlfriend."

"Oh," she groaned. "Those lap-sitters."

I talked to Bridget-Barb a little longer. She was not only a babe magnet but a butt magnet, at least any time her lap presented itself at a lesbian barbecue or potluck. "The more dykes drink," she told me, "the more they love to lap-sit." The bathroom opened and Bridget-Barb went in, but she tossed me one more tidbit as the door was closing behind her. "I start to feel like Santa Claus!"

If you're a drunken lap-sitter, be aware that this may cause dyke drama in an insecure relationship as well as future health problems in your victims, such as snaking varicose veins and—in cases of prolonged circulatory obstruction—osteoporosis and hip fractures.

If you're the frequent victim of lap-sitters, the best approach is to never sit down. Another good tactic is to sit only on objects that are either higher or considerably lower than your knees.

Remember: Never allow your thighs to be parallel to the floor. If you do allow your thighs to be parallel, crossing your legs will deter some but not all lesbian lap-sitters. Leaning against a counter, sitting cross-legged on the floor, or hugging your knees tightly to your chest are all viable options that provide rest and comfort while preventing the unwanted arrival of flirtatious bottoms.

Waiting till you see the lap-sitter coming before you stand up doesn't always work, especially not when the lap-sitter is prepared to use stealth. Keeping an eye out for lap-sitters puts the burden on you to always be aware. That doesn't sound like a very good time, does it?

Proprietary Touching

Unlike exhibitionism, which involves mutual displays of affection, the crime of proprietary touching is performed by one partner onto another. Rhonda and Tianna have just met Tracy and Sue at a lesbian potluck that consists of lawyers from Rhonda's firm and members of Tianna's bowling group. The foursome chats and laughs together until Rhonda drunkenly stumbles off to grab a brownie. At this point, under the pretense of smoothing her girlfriend's blouse, tipsy Tracy turns to Sue and begins to stroke her cleavage. *Why does she do this?* The cleavage-stroking is maintained for a while. Next Tracy begins, with a slow rhythmic arm motion, as if plucking out a love song on an invisible harp, to caress Sue's hair with her knuckles, all while continuing to relay an amusing bowling anecdote. Tianna is reminded of how Dr. Hannibal Lecter might stroke Clarissa's hair once she was bound and gagged and he was free to do as he liked, and this makes her feel like the victim of something sinister and impolite. At the same time, Sue also continues to converse with Tianna as if it's perfectly acceptable for Tracy to drift off into a creepy Sue-worship land. Sue looks like an overwrought mom at the supermarket, kids tugging on her pantleg, pleading, "Can I please have some Cocoa Puffs? Please..."

The next morning, Tianna calls her ex-girlfriend, Wynona, who had once dated Sue, and recounts the entire incident to shrieks of laughter. From then on, all Tianna, Rhonda, and

Wynona need to do to dissolve each other into puddles is simulate Tracy's version of proprietary touching.

The moral of this story? If your gal is a proprietary toucher, it's *your* responsibility to confront her about it. And the situation can only be made worse by excess consumption of alcohol. You don't want to become a couple of lesbian laughingstocks, do you? It's not likely she's aware of her behavior's creepy impact on others, and by tolerating it you're making her look bad—or just odd. Let her know you're OK with affectionate gestures but that sustained caresses of more than two to three strokes is just not cool, OK? There's something that's just too needy about that.

Perhaps your partner does this as a substitute for your own reciprocation. Turn and give her a big bone-crushing hug and say, "I love you." This may stop the behavior. A hug will at least enable you to restrain her hands and break the compulsive cycle. And it's nonthreatening! Outward signs of annoyance, such as heavy sighing, expressions of misery, or squirming, will likely increase the behavior.

If you're stuck as a captive witness to proprietary touching, proper etiquette is to immediately excuse yourself to find the bathroom or make a quick phone call to your pet sitter. This sends a passive message that proprietary touching has turned your stomach and you had to leave. Continue to leave the vicinity whenever this behavior recurs.

News flash: This is as much an etiquette book as it is a survival guide.

Conversational Exhibitionism

Imagine the two couples, Tianna and Rhonda and Tracy and Sue, in a similar scenario. Rhonda drunkenly wanders off for a brownie, and this time Tracy and Sue exhibit their sexual chemistry *for each other*. Third Wheel Syndrome is setting in fast for Tianna. She's pinching herself, wondering if she's really home watching soft porn on the *Lesbian Foreplay* channel.

"Sue has great breasts? Don't you, Sue?" asks tipsy Tracy.

"I do," answers Sue, admiring them.

"Yes, you do," says Tracy, extracting an ice cube from her gin and tonic and dropping it into Sue's cleavage.

Sue fishes into her cleavage, retrieves the ice cube, and plunks it into her mouth. Next she and Tracy commence passing the ice cube between their lips while kissing.

What should Tianna do? Stubbornly wait for them to return their attention to her? Make catcalls, throw money, and egg them on? "That's it, girls, give me a show!" Or slink off in disgust?

Well, making catcalls and egging them on is probably what they want. If it's not what they want, they will stop pretty quickly. If it's not what you want, you'd best disappear—and *fast*.

DUIs and Domestic Violence

Despite the humorous tone of this chapter, there *are* serious consequences to alcohol abuse. A couple of years ago in California, respected superior court judge Diana Hall was arrested on suspicion of drunk driving, with a blood alcohol level that would pickle a cucumber. The scandal got worse when her domestic partner, Deidra Dykeman—and no, I did *not* make up that name*—testified in court that this was the same night Judge Hall pulled her hair, bit her, and threatened to shoot her dog with a .38 caliber revolver (Hall was pacing around the house—looking for the dog?—with the gun at the

---

*I do not know if Dykeman is this woman's given name, or if she changed it during the '70s, but I would appreciate a call if anyone knows. If it was changed in the '70s, it should be Dykemon, I think, so it's probably her actual name.

time) while Dykeman made a 911 call. According to the *Los Angeles Times,* Hall was also charged with "damaging a telephone to block a 911 call," a crime I never even knew existed, which raises the question of whether there are any other times it is illegal to damage a phone, such as when I am in desperate need of a pizza.

I relate to Deidra Dykeman because I once had a violent, DUI-accumulating domestic partner. I was barely 21, before domestic partnership was even the awkward but accepted term it is today. I too had my hair pulled and was bitten. And I am here to say: Deidra, better that this should all come out now than later, better than after your precious dog turns up dead.

That being said, it is hard to be a judge, or even to judge a judge, in a world where lesbians are still supposed to be invisible.

I wish Judge Hall the best of luck.

Resources for Lesbians Who Can't Hold Their Liquor and Don't Seem to Care

www.aaws.org
www.alcholics-anonymous.org
www.sobercity.com

Dyke Drama

RECOVERY

Or, Get Thee to a Therapist!

what it
means to recover
* why is it so hard?
* formerly drama-prone
lesbians share what life is like on the
other side * tools of a super sappho
* get thee to a therapist!
* find thee a therapist!
* have a laugh

"Dyke drama can be a kind of a drug. The more you have of it, the more you want it. When you don't have it, it's like there's a void. But you have to learn to fill the void with positive things, not negative ones." —M. Schmitz

What It Means to Recover

Eventually all lesbians do recover from dyke drama. Of course, for most this only happens when they die. What it means to recover before you die is that you're only *practically* dead (quite old), but hey, you've learned to live drama-free and it feels great—even better than how you feel after a great big dose of Celebrex.

Why Is It So Hard?
All change is hard.
(But if other lesbians can do it, so can you!)

True Testimonials:
Formerly Drama-Prone Lesbians Share What Life Is Like on the Other Side

"I live in a zero-tolerance no-drama zone!" —Marilyn Jaye Lewis

"I think I used to invite dyke drama into my life. Maybe I kind of thrived on it in some sick way. Over the past year or so, though, I've mellowed out and don't want any part of it. Peace and calm are much better." —S. Ferrarri

"I used to love the rush of it, but now I'm much happier and much more centered. Anybody seen my dentures?" —C.B.

"I think I did invite dyke drama into my life. I have a very addictive sort of personality—I feed on the intense highs and lows of life. Dyke drama fed that need for intense emotion. As I've dealt with this behavior (yay, therapy!) I find I have less and less dyke drama in my life. I really just don't want it. It takes too much energy, and I don't have time to be sulking about things I can't change. Accept, learn, and move on." —Arden

"When I was younger I thought I was supposed to 'save' women. I'm much healthier now. And settled." —Adelina C.

"My partner and I lead a very sane, calm life. She theorizes this is why we have no dyke friends..." —Melissande

Note: Before-and-after photos were edited from this section as the publisher deemed them too disturbing to be printed.

-------------------------------❦-------------------------------

Tools of the Super Sappho

The Super Sappho uses four main weapons against dyke drama:

1. **She talks about it and addresses it in creative ways.** As the great feminist astrologer Caroline Casey once said, "Create theatre or live melodrama." The Super Sappho creates *period*. The aspiring drama-free lesbian may decide to write a book about her problems, or make a collage that expresses her rage over a particularly petty issue, or organize a dyke-drama poetry slam. Whatever works, OK? Whatever gets it off the ol' chest.

2. **She's out.** The Super Sappho knows she has to *be out* in order to *reach out*. If her sexual preference is a dark, dark secret—or only between herself and her tiny insular community—who can

she go to for help? Who can she go to for advice? No woman can be blackmailed with the truth if the truth is out there to begin with! Straight friends—and I mean of the humdrummest variety—can be very powerful allies. You start to tell them about all your dyke drama, and they look at you like *huh?* What could be more healing?

3. **She's in therapy.** That's right. The Super Sappho is in therapy. (What? You think she worked it out on her own with those rage collages you see posted all over her bedroom wall?)

4. **She's learned to recognize it from a distance.** And she runs like hell when she sees it coming.

Get Thee to a Therapist!

OK, but first you have to find one.

Find Thee a Therapist!

Therapists are best discovered through word-of-mouth recommendations or referrals from a trusted physician or circus performer. It's very important to shop around and to sit for several different ones first, because there are a lot out there who are just plain bad. Warning signs include: distant, cold, defensive, too effusive, or any other quality that makes you feel uncomfortable. The right therapist is someone you wouldn't mind visiting one or two times a week for a long while. An even better therapist is someone you wouldn't mind *paying* to visit one or two times a week. Because you will pay.

Find a therapist who knows what dyke drama is.

More importantly, find a therapist who knows what a dyke is.

It's a bad idea to hire a relative, a friend, a business associate, or an ex-lover as a therapist. Circus performers, and performers in general, often make bad therapists because they are attention-grabbers. However, circus (and other) performers often know really good therapists, because they often need them too.

Have a Laugh

According to the Association for Applied and Therapeutic Humor, an appreciation for the absurdities in life may enhance work performance, improve health, and facilitate emotional healing or coping. So please, have a laugh. In other words, let's stop bickering amongst ourselves and get out there and improve the world!

Acknowledgments

I'd like to offer a hymn of praise to the thoughtful women who answered my dyke drama survey. To those who offered extensive input to the earliest rough drafts, then asked not to be thanked by name, I offer this compromise: Thank you Lizzy, Miss Woo, Judy, Bobbie G., Mick, and, of course, Mom. I couldn't have written a word without my beloved stick bugs (too numerous and indistinguishable to name, but such an amazing and rapidly reproducing bunch of tiny muses there never was!). Ellen Forney's hilarious illustrations and Matt Sams's daring book and cover design added just the touch of class this book was lacking. For above-and-beyond diligence, my bulldog, Whitey, was priceless. And finally, if it weren't for Angela Brown, *Dyke Drama* would never have been possible at all.